CHALLENGING HISTORY
RESOURCE PACK

20th CENTURY DICTATORSHIPS
HITLER AND STALIN

John Traynor

Nelson

Thomas Nelson & Sons Ltd
Nelson House
Mayfield Road
Walton-on-Thames
Surrey KT12 5PL
United Kingdom

© John Traynor

First published by Thomas Nelson & Sons Ltd 1999

ISBN: 0-17-435203-4
9 8 7 6 5 4 3 2 1
03 02 01 99 99

Production team
Commissioning and development: Steve Berry
Cover design: Michael Fay
Book design and illustration: Jordan Publishing Design
Editorial: Lynne Williamson
Photo research: Image Select International

Printed in the UK by Antony Rowe Ltd, Chippenham

Photograph acknowledgements
The publishers are grateful to the following for permission to reproduce photographs:
AKG pages 15, 22; Bildarchiv Preussischer Kulturbesitz page 10; Hulton Getty pages 4, 6, 14, 21, 24, 27, 29, 32, 38, 40.

Contents

Preview

As an A level student you will already know a great deal about Hitler and Stalin. The chances are that the focus of your attention has been the periods 1928–53 in the case of Stalin, and between 1933–45 for Hitler. In this unit we will examine some of the less well-known aspects of their early lives. It may be that in so doing we can detect signs of the characteristics which became so pronounced when the dictators entered public life. For example, a brief glance at one moment in Stalin's early career – a combination of Bolshevik and, according to some sources, bank robber – might later help you to understand why he was so well equipped to emerge triumphant in the power struggle of 1924–28.

In the winter of 1903–4, Stalin (or 'Koba' as he was then known) was in exile at Novaia Uda, 230 km beyond the last stop on the Trans-Siberian Railway. Temperatures of minus 40 degrees, biting winds and a bleak landscape would have made most people think twice about stepping outside, let alone trying to escape. But Koba was made of stern stuff. In December 1903 he attempted an escape but was driven back by frostbite. However, Koba possessed an implacable will and even the prospect of further exposure to the harshest conditions on earth was not enough to make him give up. He returned to Novaia Uda for more clothes and then set out into the wilderness again on 5 January 1904. This time Koba was able to secure the services of a sledge driver who agreed to transport him in return for a supply of vodka. It took six weeks to reach the railway at Irkutsk. In escaping from his captors, Koba had displayed the fighting qualities which would stand him in good stead throughout his political life.

One of the most striking features of Hitler and Stalin appears in their fanatical attachment to particular political beliefs. Hitler's racial theories and Stalin's commitment to communism became central to the political careers of these dictators. This unit examines the formative years of the dictators. When did they develop the convictions which later meant so much to them? What was the significance of their background, upbringing and environment? Finally, what light has been shed on the early lives of the dictators by the recent investigations of historians?

Card from the register of the Tsarist secret police of St Petersburg with photographs of Stalin.

Challenging History Resource Pack. Text © John Traynor; Illustrations © Thomas Nelson & Sons Ltd; Photographs © as listed on p.2, sourced texts on p.44. Published by Thomas Nelson & Sons Ltd 1999.

Hitler's formative years

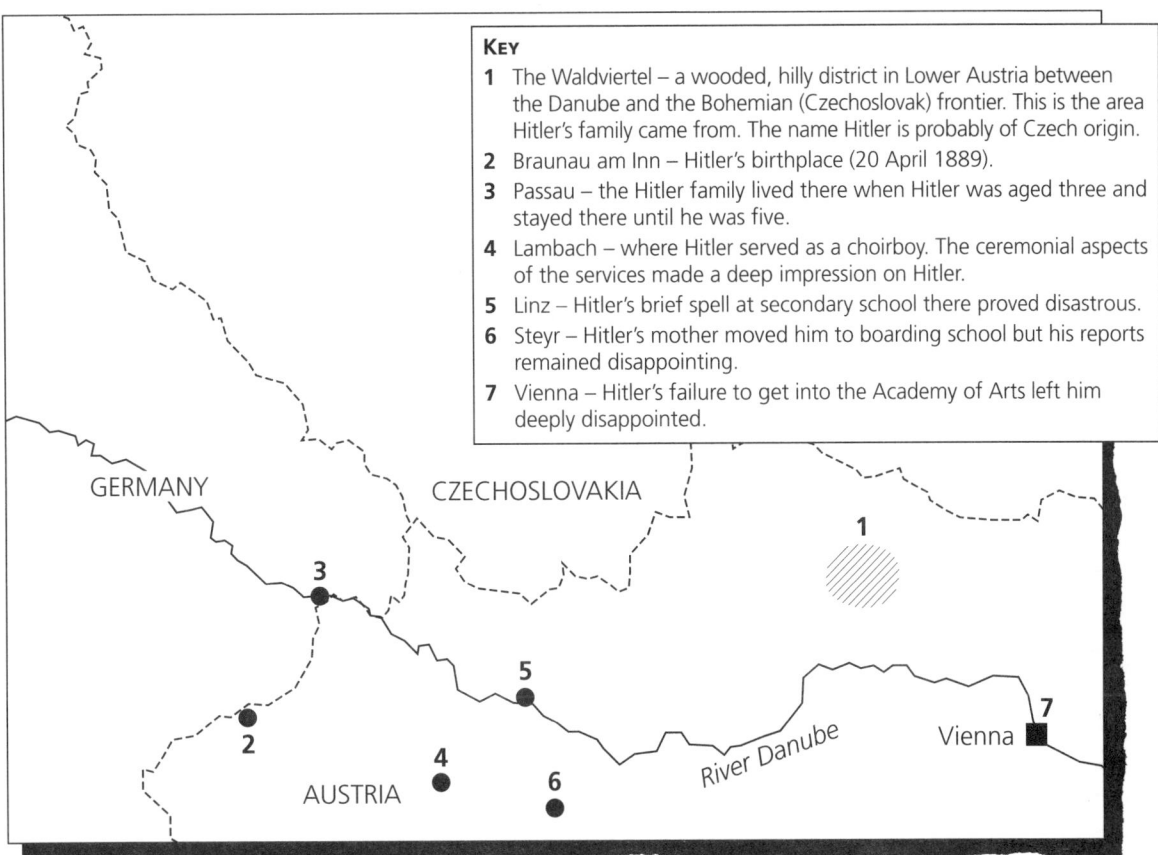

KEY

1 The Waldviertel – a wooded, hilly district in Lower Austria between the Danube and the Bohemian (Czechoslovak) frontier. This is the area Hitler's family came from. The name Hitler is probably of Czech origin.
2 Braunau am Inn – Hitler's birthplace (20 April 1889).
3 Passau – the Hitler family lived there when Hitler was aged three and stayed there until he was five.
4 Lambach – where Hitler served as a choirboy. The ceremonial aspects of the services made a deep impression on Hitler.
5 Linz – Hitler's brief spell at secondary school there proved disastrous.
6 Steyr – Hitler's mother moved him to boarding school but his reports remained disappointing.
7 Vienna – Hitler's failure to get into the Academy of Arts left him deeply disappointed.

Stalin's formative years

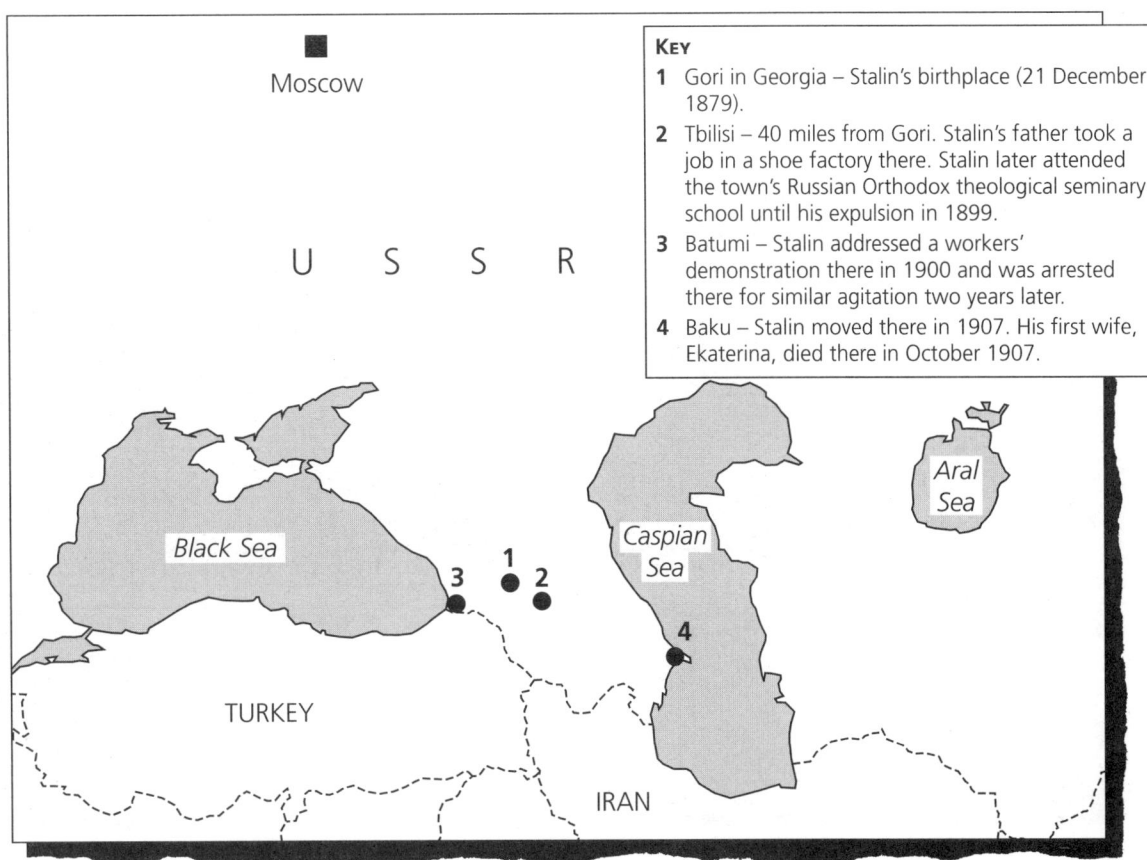

KEY

1 Gori in Georgia – Stalin's birthplace (21 December 1879).
2 Tbilisi – 40 miles from Gori. Stalin's father took a job in a shoe factory there. Stalin later attended the town's Russian Orthodox theological seminary school until his expulsion in 1899.
3 Batumi – Stalin addressed a workers' demonstration there in 1900 and was arrested there for similar agitation two years later.
4 Baku – Stalin moved there in 1907. His first wife, Ekaterina, died there in October 1907.

Challenging History Resource Pack. Text © John Traynor; Illustrations © Thomas Nelson & Sons Ltd; Photographs © as listed on p.2, sourced texts on p.44. Published by Thomas Nelson & Sons Ltd 1999.

Age	HITLER

0–10

1889

Born on 20 April in Braunau am Inn, a small Austrian town close to the Bavarian border with Germany. Adolf was the third child of Alois Hitler's third marriage. The two older children died in infancy and of a total of five children, only Adolf and a younger sister, Paula, survived into adulthood. His father Alois was a stern, bad-tempered, authoritarian figure. However, his job as a customs official was well paid and Adolf enjoyed a comfortable upbringing. His mother Klara was 28 when Adolf was born, whereas Alois was already in his fifties. The family moved several times and Adolf attended three different primary schools.

At the age of eight Adolf became a chorister in the monastery school at Lambach. He was deeply impressed with the spectacle of the services. At this point Adolf's school career appeared to be going reasonably well but after two years there was a further move to a school at Leonding. This was followed within a year by a move to secondary school.

11

1900

Hitler was admitted to the Linz Realschule. Adolf's work deteriorated, as did his behaviour and attitude. Socially isolated, his only talent appeared to be drawing. Within a year he was asked to leave. His mother moved him to a boarding school in Steyr but his performance did not improve.

13

1903

Alois died on 3 January. Hitler does not appear to have been close to his father. Klara (now aged 42) moved Adolf and his sister Paula to Linz. Hitler befriended August Kubizek. Together they attended the Linz theatre and were spellbound by the Wagnerian opera.

16

1905

Adolf suffered from a lung infection in the summer. His mother agreed that he should be allowed to leave school and apply to the Vienna Academy of Arts. Adolf used the lung infection as an excuse to defer his application until 1907.

17

1906

Adolf made his first visit to Vienna but could not settle down to any occupation or routine.

Age	HITLER

18

1907

Adolf's first application to the Vienna Academy of Arts was rejected. This demoralising blow was compounded by the news that Adolf's mother was critically ill with breast cancer. Adolf returned home to help nurse his mother. She died on 21 December 1907. Hitler was traumatised by this event. The contrast with his muted reaction to his father's death is very striking.

19

1908

Early in the year Adolf returned to Vienna.

October Adolf made a second application to the Vienna Academy of Arts. He was again rejected. This made Hitler extremely bitter.

20

November 1909

A shortage of money obliged Hitler to move out of furnished rooms and into a men's hostel near the Meidling station. At the end of the year he moved to a hostel at Meldemannstrasse. He had now reached his lowest ebb, facing what Bullock calls 'the social humiliation of the spoiled young man from a middle-class home reduced to the status of a tramp'.

21–24

1910 to 1913

Hitler remained in Viennese dosshouses, eking out money through the sale of paintings to tourists and advertising posters for small shops.

24

May 1913

Hitler left Vienna and moved to Munich. He was bitter, workshy, moody and virulently anti-Semitic. He may have moved to avoid service in the Austrian army with its large Czech element.

25

1914

1 August A photograph shows Hitler in the cheering crowd at the Odeons Platz in Munich, which had gathered to listen to the proclamation of war. Two days later Hitler volunteered to join the List Regiment. In October the regiment reached the Western Front.

Hitler in the crowd at the Odeons Platz, 1914.

Challenging History Resource Pack. Text © John Traynor; Illustrations © Thomas Nelson & Sons Ltd; Photographs © as listed on p.2, sourced texts on p.44. Published by Thomas Nelson & Sons Ltd 1999.

Age	STALIN

0–3 1879
Born on 9 December in Gori, Georgia. Lived for the first three years in a rough, brick-made hovel. Christened Iosif (known as 'Soso'). His father, Vissarion Dzhugashvili, was a tough, hard-drinking cobbler. His mother Ekatereina had lost two children in infancy and tried hard to build a life for Soso, amid acute poverty. It seems that Soso's mother was frequently beaten by Vissarion, so the boy was exposed to extreme violence from an early age.

4–8 1883
Soso probably spent some time living in the home of an Orthodox priest named Charkviani. This clergyman probably exerted considerable influence over Soso, whose mother acted as Charkviani's housekeeper.
    Meanwhile, Soso survived an attack of smallpox, blood poisoning, and being struck by a carriage which permanently damaged his left arm. When Soso was five, Vissarion left to work in a shoe factory in Tbilisi. Later Stalin wrote that his father was a decent artisan who had been obliged to join the ranks of the proletariat, and implied that disillusionment at the exploitation of factory workers led to his absorption of socialist ideals.

9 1888
Soso was enrolled by his mother in a clerical elementary school in Gori.

10 1889
Vissarion took his son to Tbilisi where he probably worked as a helper in the shoe factory for around a year. Soso's mother's will ultimately prevailed. Soso returned to Gori.

13 1892
Soso watched a public hanging, exposing him to the brutality of some aspects of Georgian life.

14 September 1894
Soso was enrolled in Tbilisi's Russian Orthodox theological seminary school where he was to study for the priesthood for almost five years. Soso became progressively more disillusioned with the school's authorities. Although a native Georgian, with a distinctive accent and culture, Soso was now obliged to learn Russian.

16–17 1896
Soso was caught reading translated copies of forbidden western books.
    Soso now became an illicit member of a 'talking circle' which discussed political ideas. His radical ideas were now taking him way beyond the boundaries of what was planned for him in the seminary school.

18 1898
Soso became a member of the Third Group, an organisation committed to direct political action rather than mere talk. He now adopted the nickname 'Koba', after a nationalist hero in a Georgian novel.

19 May 1899
Koba was expelled from seminary school for reading illicit books and for criticising college authorities. He was dismissive of the religious values which the authorities in the seminary school had tried to instil.

21 1901
January Records reveal that Koba was working in Tbilisi's Physical Institute in a clerical capacity.
March Koba's mounting political activity led him to go underground in an effort to avoid detection by the authorities.
May Following a May Day demonstration in 1900, Koba played a key role in a violent industrial dispute which led to a confrontation with the authorities and resulted in serious casualties.
November Left Tbilisi and went to Batumi.

Age	STALIN

22 April 1902
Arrested in Batumi after instigating a workers' demonstration. Held in jail until the autumn and then exiled to Siberia for three years.

23 November 1903
Held in Siberia until he escaped in January 1904. Frostbite forced him to abandon the first escape bid, but he later made his way across the frozen wastes to Transcaucasia where he resumed his work as a member of the revolutionary underground.

25 1905
Married Ekaterina Svanidze, reluctantly agreeing to a church wedding.
    Praised by Lenin for an article he had written.
December Met Lenin for the first time at the Bolshevik conference in Finland.

26 1906
Koba made his first speech at the Stockholm Party Congress. His speech was short but his performance was confident.

27 1907
March His first child, Yakov, was born.
April to May Visited London for party congress.
April Published his first major article, 'Anarchism or Socialism?'.
October Death of his first wife.

28 March 1908
Arrested in Baku after four years on the run from the authorities. He spent seven months in prison and was then exiled to Solvychegodsk.

29 June 1909
Escaped from exile and returned to underground politics. Tried to organise a strike in the oil fields of Baku.

30 March 1910
Arrested and later returned to exile in Solvychegodsk.

31 1911
Allowed to reside in Volgoda.
September Arrested after an illegal visit to St. Petersburg. Held in prison until December and then returned to Volgoda.

32 1912
February Left Volgoda illegally for St. Petersburg.
Spring Koba was co-opted to the newly created Bolshevik Central Committee.
April Arrested in St. Petersburg and exiled to Narym, Siberia.
August Absconded from lodgings and returned again to St. Petersburg. He worked on the Bolshevik paper *Pravda* and used the name 'K. Stalin' for the first time, to accompany a short article. Visited Cracow and met with Lenin.

33 1913
Wrote an essay on 'Marxism and the National Question'.
February Arrested shortly after his return to St. Petersburg. The authorities were tired of Stalin's escape bids and this time he was sent to a remote, frozen section of northern Siberia.

36 1916
Towards the end of the year Stalin was given an army medical but rejected because of his withered left arm. Stalin's career within the party had stalled and a letter to Lenin suggesting publication of his essays came to nothing.

37 March 1917
Released from exile in Siberia following the abdication of Nicholas II, Stalin was elected to the editorial board of *Pravda*.

Challenging History Resource Pack. Text © John Traynor; Illustrations © Thomas Nelson & Sons Ltd; Photographs © as listed on p.2, sourced texts on p.44. Published by Thomas Nelson & Sons Ltd 1999.

Contemporary sources

HITLER

Source A

During these years a view of life and a definite outlook on the world took shape in my mind. These became the granite basis of my conduct at that time. Since then I have extended that foundation very little, I have changed nothing in it…Vienna was a hard school for me, but it taught me the most profound lessons of my life.

Adolf Hitler, *Mein Kampf* (1925)

Source C

The idea of struggle is as old as life itself, for life is only preserved because other living things perish through struggle…In this struggle, the stronger, the more able win, while the less able, the weak lose.

Extract from a speech made by Hitler at Kulmbach, 5 February 1928

Source B

One day when passing through the Inner City, I suddenly encountered a phenomenon in a long caftan and wearing black sidelocks. My first thought was: is this a Jew?…But the longer I gazed at this strange countenance and examined it section by section, the more the question shaped itself in my brain: is this a German? I turned to books for help in removing my doubts. For the first time in my life I bought myself some anti-Semitic pamphlets for a few pence…

As soon as I began to investigate the matter…Vienna appeared to me in a new light…Was there any shady undertaking, any form of foulness, especially in cultural life, in which at least one Jew did not participate? On putting the probing knife to that kind of abscess one immediately discovered, like a maggot in a putrescent body, a little Jew who was often blinded by the sudden light.

Adolf Hitler, *Mein Kampf* (1925)

STALIN

Source D

It is difficult to describe the process. First one becomes convinced that existing conditions are wrong and unjust. Then one resolves to do the best one can to remedy them. Under the Tsar's regime any attempt genuinely to help the people put one outside the pale of the law; one found himself hunted and hounded as a revolutionist.

Stalin talking to American interviewer Jerome Davis in 1926 taken from Robert H. McNeal, *Stalin: Man and Ruler* (1988)

Source E

I joined the revolutionary movement when 15 years old, when I became connected with underground groups of Russian Marxists then living in Transcaucasia. These groups exerted great influence on me and instilled a taste for underground Marxist literature.

Extract from an interview with Stalin in 1934, taken from Robert H. McNeal, *Stalin: Man and Ruler* (1988)

TASKS

1   What problems does an examination of the early lives of the dictators present for historians?

2   What do you consider to be the key moments in the early lives of Hitler and Stalin?

3   Summarise the formative ideas of Stalin. At what point in Stalin's life would you say he had acquired his basic political outlook? Repeat this exercise in the case of Hitler.

4   To what extent is the account provided by Hitler of his formative anti-Semitism accepted by the historians whose views are presented here?

5   How far would you agree with the view that a lack of conclusive, reliable evidence on the early lives of the dictators makes it unwise to draw any firm conclusions?

The views of historians

HITLER

Source F

The essence of Hitler's personal world-view comprised a belief in history as racial struggle, radical anti-Semitism, a conviction that Germany's future could be secured only through conquest of Lebensraum (Living Space) at the expense of Russia and the uniting of all these strands in the notion of a life-or-death fight to the finish with Marxism…Exactly when, how and why Hitler's fanatically held ideas took their hold on him is far from clear. But the gradual forging of the various strands of his thinking into a composite ideology was completed by the time of the writing of *Mein Kampf* in 1929, and scarcely wavered thereafter.

Ian Kershaw, *Hitler: Profiles in Power* (1991)

Source H

For most of his Vienna years he had no independently thought-out political line. Rather, he was filled with emotions of hatred and defensiveness…Alongside these were vague, up welling prejudices against Jews and other minorities…He was obsessed by fears of Jews and Slavs…His fellows in the home for men did not share his paranoid emotions…

In retrospect, Hitler laid claim to an intense intellectual development. During the approximately five years he spent in Vienna, he maintained, he read 'enormously and thoroughly'…But it would probably be more accurate to say that the real influences of this phase of his life stemmed not so much from the intellectual realm as from that of demagogy and political tactics…His experiences during this phase of his life helped Hitler arrive at that philosophy of struggle that became the central core of his view of the world…his belief in brutal struggle, in harshness, cruelty, destruction, the rights of the stranger…He learned in that school for meanness in Vienna.

Joachim C. Fest, *Hitler* (1974)

Source G

We remain in the dark about why Hitler became a manic anti-Semite…Hitler's own story, retailed in *Mein Kampf*, tells of his conversion to anti-Semitism after encountering a Kaftan-garbed figure with black hair locks in the streets of Vienna. This was probably a dramatisation. Hitler was already reading pan-German anti-Semitic newspapers in his Linz days and was even then an admirer of the Austrian anti-Semite and pan-German leader Georg von Schorerer.

Ian Kershaw, *Hitler: Profiles in Power* (1991)

Source I

Hitler's early life, unlike Stalin's was not one of hardship and poverty. Contrary to the impression he portrays in *Mein Kampf*, he was neither poor nor harshly treated. His father…had a secure income, as well as the social standing of an imperial official, and when he died he left his widow and children well provided for.

Alan Bullock, *Hitler and Stalin: Parallel Lives* (1991)

Source J

The picture which Hitler gives of Vienna in *Mein Kampf* is not correct. He says that he became an anti-Semite in Vienna, but if you check the contemporary sources closely, you see that, on the contrary, he was very good friends with very many, extraordinarily many Jews, both in the men's hostel and through his contact with the dealers who sold his pictures.

Brigitte Hamann, *Hitler's Wein* (1996)

STALIN

Source K

He was, in fact, descended from peasants on both sides. His parents were illiterate, or semi-literate at best…Two children died at birth before Stalin was born. He himself nearly died at the age of five from smallpox, which left his face pockmarked. His left arm was permanently injured as a result of a childhood accident…His father was a rough, violent man who drank heavily, beat his wife and child, and found it hard to make a living…he bitterly resented his father's treatment of him but it did not break his spirit.

Alan Bullock, *Hitler and Stalin: Parallel Lives* (1991)

Source L

It is impossible to determine exactly when the seminarian transferred his allegiance to Marxism…Quite possibly, the first contacts with radicals were in a book shop…a place frequented by young intellectuals, including seminarians, Djugashvili among them.

Robert H. McNeal, *Stalin: Man and Ruler* (1988)

HITLER and STALIN

Source M

Neither belonged to the traditional ruling class and it is difficult to imagine either coming to power in the world into which they were born. Their careers were possible only in the new world created by the breakdown of the old order in Europe, as a result of the First World War…Yet their ideas and beliefs were formed and remained set in the mould of the world in which they grew up. Stalin's Marxism, Hitler's combination of Social Darwinism and racism were nineteenth-century systems which reached the peak of their influence in Europe at the turn of the century, in the last decade of the nineteenth century, and the first of the twentieth century.

Alan Bullock, *Hitler and Stalin: Parallel Lives* (1991)

Challenging History Resource Pack. Text © John Traynor; Illustrations © Thomas Nelson & Sons Ltd; Photographs © as listed on p.2, sourced texts on p.44. Published by Thomas Nelson & Sons Ltd 1999.

Preview

A right-wing demonstration in Munich in 1919.

Hitler derived intense personal satisfaction from his wartime service in the List Regiment. In the words of one of his superiors, 'the List Regiment was his homeland'. For the first time since his mother's death, Hitler felt a sense of belonging. Hitler's biographer Joachim Fest writes that life in the army gave Hitler a sense of prestige, while its impersonality suited his temperament. His solitary work as a messenger carrier between the regimental staff and the front line trenches meant that he retained his sense of isolation and his eccentric, brooding mannerisms. Nevertheless, several accounts testify to Hitler's bravery, loyalty and willingness to obey even the most dangerous of orders. Despite these qualities, Hitler was never promoted beyond the rank of private, first class. His adjutant later recalled that Hitler had not displayed 'leadership qualities' and added that Hitler himself had not wanted promotion.

Hitler was, in his own way, contented but this almost idyllic period was abruptly shattered in the autumn of 1918. The acute sense of trauma which accompanied his mother's death was to return in the most painful of circumstances. On the night of 13 October Hitler's regiment faced a British gas attack at Wervick, near Ypres. Within hours, exposure to mustard gas had taken away Hitler's sight. He later recalled that 'my eyes had turned into glowing coals'. The hysterical and deeply shocked young soldier was taken to the Pasewalk hospital in Pomerania, where his eyesight gradually returned. However, for Hitler worse was to follow. He was still in hospital when on 10 November 1918 he was informed that a revolution had broken out in Germany and that the Kaiser had abdicated. In his own words: 'since the day I had stood at my mother's grave, I had not wept…but now I could not help it.' The news of Germany's imminent defeat traumatised Hitler. Contentment had been replaced by deep despair. The next day the war, and with it Hitler's sense of purpose, came to an end.

At the end of the war Hitler appeared to be a lost soul. The news of Germany's defeat was almost impossible for him to accept. Yet within a year Hitler found a new sense of direction as he stumbled into the political arena, albeit on its most extreme fringes. How was it possible for this socially isolated, obsessive young man to become the most important member of a political party which would eventually become the largest in German history?

This unit will enable you to examine Hitler's development of his position, from a mere observer of the German Workers' Party in September 1919, to its dominant figure at the time of the Munich Beer-Hall Putsch in November 1923.

Challenging History Resource Pack. Text © John Traynor; Illustrations © Thomas Nelson & Sons Ltd; Photographs © as listed on p.2, sourced texts on p.44. Published by Thomas Nelson & Sons Ltd 1999.

Hitler's rise to dominance within his own party

November 1918

Following his release from Pasewalk hospital and his recovery from the gas attack which had temporarily blinded him, Hitler made his way to Munich. The city was in turmoil amid the trauma of defeat, and a once cosmopolitan and tolerant place became a seething stamping ground for bitter, demobilised soldiers and a variety of extremist cranks.

9 January 1919

Railway mechanic Anton Drexler set up the German Workers' Party (DAP) which, as Fest puts it, 'was very small potatoes'. Initial membership was between twenty to forty people.

Spring 1919

The army retained Hitler's services at the end of the war and assigned him to an 'educational unit'. Based at a barracks at Camp Lachfeld, Hitler attended a series of army indoctrination courses and made an impression on other course members with his strongly held views. It was at this point that Hitler first experienced the thrill of seeing groups of people respond to his crude, emotional language and imagery. Hitler was now used as an agent with the task of investigating the various political parties which were springing up amid the chaos of post-war Germany.

August 1919

Hitler made his first public comments on the 'Jewish Question' in a 'lecture' to demobilised soldiers, organised by the Reichswehr.

September 1919

Hitler attended a meeting of the DAP. He spoke out at the end of the meeting and was subsequently sent a membership card inviting him to become the 555th person to join. After a few days, Hitler decided to join and became the 7th member of the party's board. At that point the party was just one of more than 70 similar political groups on the extreme right wing of German politics.

Hitler returned to his barracks and eagerly set about typing letters and making contacts. He immediately devoted more time to the party than the majority of the other members.

In the same month Hitler set out his first detailed political statement in a letter which contained his early views on anti-Semitism. Before the year was over, Hitler had become the party's propaganda chief.

16 October 1919

Hitler delivered a blistering speech at the party's first public meeting. Afterwards, Hitler had discovered 'I could speak'. Before the end of the year the party had moved into headquarters – a rented room in the Sternecker beer hall. Hitler was dragging the party forward, out of complete obscurity and onto the edge of the public arena.

24 February 1920

At the Hofbrauhaus in Munich the party announced details of a 25-point programme which Hitler had helped to create. Within a week the party changed its name from the German Workers' Party to the National Socialist German Workers' Party (NSDAP), or Nazi Party for short, and adopted the swastika as its battle symbol. Hitler's artistic talents were now employed in designing posters and publicity material for party meetings.

31 March 1920

Hitler left the Reichswehr and devoted his energies to politics, although his friendship with Ernst Rohm enabled Hitler to retain a useful contact with the army. In a series of speeches over the next few months, Hitler repeatedly condemned the Jews in the most extreme terms. Hitler was now developing a link between the Jews and Bolshevism, contending that weak government and poor social conditions in Germany were playing into the hands of the revolutionary Marxists, whom he connected with Soviet Russia and World Jewry. Hitler, with his talent for crude simplification and his ability to connect with his beer hall audience, was becoming the most effective speaker in the party. This set him apart from party 'intellectuals' such as Gottfried Feder and Alfred Rosenberg, who lacked Hitler's emotionally raw appeal.

December 1920

The NSDAP bought the newspaper the *Munchener Beobachter*, which was then renamed the *Volkischer Beobachter* (this became the party's daily newspaper from February 1923).

July 1921

Hitler responded to policy differences within the party by offering his resignation on 11 July. He issued preconditions for his return and these were accepted at a meeting at the end of July which saw Hitler emerge as Party Chairman with dictatorial powers.

Challenging History Resource Pack. Text © John Traynor; Illustrations © Thomas Nelson & Sons Ltd; Photographs © as listed on p.2, sourced texts on p.44. Published by Thomas Nelson & Sons Ltd 1999.

3 August 1921

The armed squads which provided protection for party members were formally organised into what was euphemistically called the 'Gymnastic and Sports Section' and which in October was renamed the 'Storm Detachments' (SA). The SA was deployed to prevent disruption of party meetings and to intimidate political opponents.

February 1922

Hitler made a speech to the SA in which he claimed that the 'Jewish Question' was his 'single, total and exclusive' concern.

May 1922

There were 45 party branches, mostly in Bavaria and many beyond the direct control of Hitler. By late 1922, total membership was around 20,000.

Summer 1922

By the time of the murder of the Jewish German Foreign Minister Walter Rathenau, the NSDAP's violent tendencies meant that the party had been outlawed in virtually every German state, with the notable exception of Bavaria. In July, Hitler was briefly imprisoned after violence at an opposition meeting the previous September. By now Hitler was consciously developing his own personality cult amongst his loyal followers.

10 October 1922

Hitler's esteem was boosted by the decision of Julius Streicher to merge his *volkisch* group, based in Nuremberg, with the NSDAP under Hitler's leadership.

December 1922

Historian Ian Kershaw states that by now, Hitler had formulated the basis of his personalised world-view, namely, 'the struggle to destroy the power of international Jewry, the struggle to annihilate Marxism, and the struggle to obtain "living space" for Germany at the expense of Russia'.

January 1923

The party organised its first 'Reich Party Rally' in Munich. Speakers at the rally condemned the Weimar government's weakness in the face of the French and Belgian occupation of the Ruhr. The sense of crisis which this created eventually led Hitler to decide that he could attempt a national uprising.

February 1923

The SA joined with other Bavarian paramilitary groups and became increasingly militarised.

1 March 1923

The SA was placed under the command of Hermann Goering. By late 1923, party membership had reached nearly 50,000.

November 1923

The Munich Beer-Hall Putsch. Hitler led a march through Munich which he hoped would lead to the overthrow of the Bavarian Government and to the proclamation of a national revolution. The putsch dissolved amid a hail of gunfire from the Bavarian authorities. Hitler had seriously over-estimated his own position. Sixteen of his followers were killed. Hitler fled the scene but was subsequently arrested.

26 February 1924

Hitler and his colleagues went on trial for high treason at a court in Munich. During the trial Hitler launched a spirited defence of his actions. He now presented himself as an anti-Marxist. Hitler received considerable press coverage, much of it favourable. Although the putsch had ended in calamity, Hitler had managed to turn the trial into a personal triumph, consolidating his position as the dominant figure in the party and establishing himself as the key political figure of the extreme right.

1 April 1924

Hitler was fined 200 gold marks and sentenced to five years in prison in Landsberg am Lech, where he wrote *Mein Kampf* (*My Struggle*). He was released on 20 December after serving less than a year in prison. By the time Hitler emerged from prison it was clear that he was indispensable to the party. During his imprisonment the party, under the stand-in leadership of Rosenberg, had virtually disintegrated, completely losing the momentum it had enjoyed until the abortive putsch and splitting into various rival factions. Without Hitler's leadership the party was dead in the water.

TASKS

1 Look at the twelve factors which enabled Hitler to become the dominant figure in his party. In each case try to find evidence in the chronology of these factors at work. For example, when did Hitler display tactical awareness or deploy his artistic talents for the party cause?

2 Work in pairs to place the factors into three categories:
   (a) of major importance;
   (b) of some importance;
   (c) of marginal importance.

3 What problems did Hitler face during the period 1918–24? How successful was he in dealing with them?

4 What limitations did Hitler face when he emerged from prison in 1924?

Challenging History Resource Pack. Text © John Traynor; Illustrations © Thomas Nelson & Sons Ltd; Photographs © as listed on p.2, sourced texts on p.44. Published by Thomas Nelson & Sons Ltd 1999.

Factors which enabled Hitler to become the dominant figure in the NSDAP

❶ Hitler seems to have been able to instil a deep sense of personal loyalty into a close-knit group of 'fellow fighters' from the very early days of the party.

❷ His personal charisma – those who were not susceptible to this would tend to be outside the party.

❸ His unique talent for communication and public speaking.

❹ Hitler showed good tactical awareness in dealing with splits in the party.

❺ Hitler was able to devote unlimited time and energy to the party. Many other members had full-time jobs which prevented them from doing this.

❻ His will-power and ability to radiate a sense of purpose and drive.

❼ His understanding of propaganda techniques.

❽ His ability to out-manoeuvre rivals within the party.

❾ The failure of other figures in the party to take advantage of Hitler's imprisonment to stake their own claims to the party leadership.

❿ The popularity of his extreme ideas with the rank and file of the party membership.

⓫ His drive to organise and extend the scope of the party.

⓬ His artistic talents.

Challenging History Resource Pack. Text © John Traynor; Illustrations © Thomas Nelson & Sons Ltd; Photographs © as listed on p.2, sourced texts on p.44. Published by Thomas Nelson & Sons Ltd 1999.

Preview

Lenin died from a cerebral haemorrhage on 21 January 1924. His body was taken from his country estate at Gorki and transported by train to the Pavletsk station in Moscow. Then he was moved across Moscow to the Hall of Columns in the House of Unions where his body would lie in state until the funeral. It took three and a half days for half a million people to file past the body. With an exceptionally severe frost, the temperature overnight fell to minus 35 degrees Celsius. Bonfires were lit to warm the crowds of mourners and the

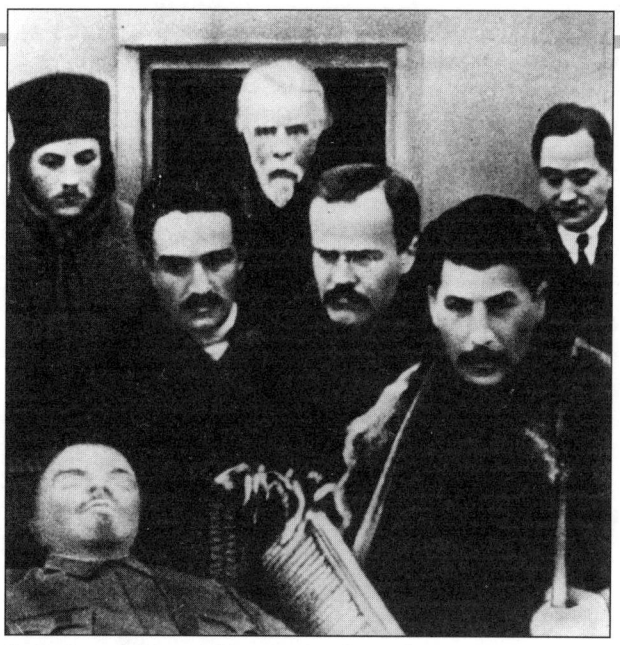

Stalin (second from left) at Lenin's funeral.

smoke from the fires combined with the frozen breath of the crowds created an extraordinary scene.

On 27 January Stalin, Zinoviev and six ordinary workers were given the honour of carrying the coffin to Red Square. Stalin was one of a group of eight politicians who lowered the coffin into its vault. Meanwhile, his rival Trotsky was ill and had been advised in a telegram to remain in Georgia. He was a notable absentee from the funeral. It was one of many errors of judgement which Trotsky would make at the start of a power struggle which, although he did not yet realise it, had already begun. Nevertheless, at the time of Lenin's death Trotsky's fame and prestige was immense. A memorial article written by Trotsky was published in *Pravda* on 24 January. The newspaper did not carry Stalin's piece until 12 February. To many, both within and outside the Communist Party, this might have been seen as an accurate indication of their relative standing.

This unit examines how it was possible for the man who appeared to many to be Lenin's most gifted and natural successor to be hounded out of the Soviet Union by a man described by one colleague as a 'grey blur', and who many considered to be a mediocrity.

TROTSKY

Background

Trotsky – born Lev Davidovich Bronstein – was the same age as Stalin. Whereas Stalin was born into poverty, Trotsky had been brought up in comfortable circumstances on a farm in Yanovka. In his early political career he had been associated with Lenin, but following the breach of 1903 he had followed the path of the Mensheviks. For more than a decade Trotsky had been one of Lenin's most outspoken critics. Trotsky established a reputation as an outstanding writer and thinker. When he returned from Western exile after the February Revolution had unseated the Tsar, he was still outside the ranks of the Bolshevik Party. However, he then transferred his allegiance in a way which was not appreciated amongst the ranks of the older Bolsheviks. Although he was arrested shortly after his return, Trotsky now said he was committed to the Bolshevik cause. His radical line enabled him to be enrolled as a Bolshevik and he quickly became a member of the party's inner committee.

Challenging History Resource Pack. Text © John Traynor; Illustrations © Thomas Nelson & Sons Ltd; Photographs © as listed on p.2, sourced texts on p.44. Published by Thomas Nelson & Sons Ltd 1999.

September 1917

Released from jail, Trotsky was then appointed from the Petrograd Soviet as Chairman of the Central Executive Committee of the Bolshevik Party. Trotsky's rapid promotion, brash self-confidence and vitriolic tongue did not endear him to Bolsheviks like Stalin.

24 October 1917

It was a sign of Lenin's confidence in Trotsky that he was made Chairman of the Military Revolutionary Committee of the Petrograd Soviet. Trotsky was placed in supreme command of the military side of the Bolshevik uprising. From his headquarters in the Smolny Institute, Trotsky issued the directives which set in motion the successful October Revolution. He had been a member of the party for less than six months. When the revolution succeeded in ousting the Provisional Government, Lenin rewarded Trotsky with the prestigious cabinet post of People's Commissar for Foreign Affairs.

January 1918

As Commissar for Foreign Affairs, Trotsky travelled to Brest-Litovsk to conduct peace negotiations with Germany. En route, Trotsky told Russian soldiers that 'the Russian Revolution will not bow its head before German imperialism'. Trotsky's command of the German language, his outstanding intellect and his gift for rhetoric enabled him to make a considerable impact on the German delegation. He produced a startling formula for 'neither peace nor war' in which Russia would not continue with the war but would refuse to sign a punitive peace treaty. However, Stalin bluntly observed that 'the position of Comrade Trotsky represents no policy at all'. Stalin's sense of realism was reflected in the fact that in March 1918, Russia was obliged to sign away one third of her territory. Trotsky resigned as Commissar for Foreign Affairs so that he would not have to bear the stigma of personally signing the treaty. Meanwhile he had moved into the Tsar's former quarters in the Kremlin.

15 January 1918

A new directive created the Red Army which Trotsky, as Commissar for War, was charged with shaping into an effective fighting unit. Trotsky realised that the raw recruits to this army were wild and poorly disciplined. He took immediate measures to reform the Red Army on the model of the old imperial one, calling up former Tsarist officers and later introducing mass conscription.

September 1918

The leadership set up the Revolutionary Military Council of the Republic which acquired massive importance, not least because the whole economy was now geared towards the winning of the Civil War. Trotsky directed the Council, but Lenin and Stalin were also members.

October 1918

Trotsky sent a telegram to Lenin criticising Stalin's conduct in the Civil War and 'insisting categorically on Stalin's recall'. Trotsky was now directing the Civil War from an armoured train. The train was lavishly equipped and included its own high-class restaurant, although at the same time many of Trotsky's troops were malnourished. Trotsky prided himself as a dapper dresser – his pre-occupation with his own meticulous appearance jarred somewhat as the leader of a fighting force 'half-starved, half-naked and half-shod', and was criticised in some quarters as 'aristocratism'. Trotsky dismissed his critics as 'party ignoramuses'.

January 1920

Trotsky was appointed Commissar for Transport. His work in the Civil War made him realise the importance of a decent railway system.

September 1922

Lenin proposed to counter Stalin's increasingly powerful position by offering Trotsky the post of his deputy in the Council of People's Commissars (Sovnarkom). Trotsky 'categorically refused' the post, probably because his pride was affronted at the thought of being merely a deputy chairman. Stalin made political capital out of Trotsky's 'arrogant' refusal.

Autumn 1923

Trotsky launched his first concerted criticisms of the triumvirate (Stalin, Zinoviev and Kamenev). On 15 October a bloc of 46 party members issued a statement containing ideological criticisms of the new leadership. In addition, Trotsky wrote two open letters to the Central Committee suggesting a 'New Course'. This was criticised by Stalin and his supporters. Then, at the end of October, Trotsky picked up a malarial infection during a hunting expedition. The illness debilitated him at a critical time.

21 January 1924

Lenin's death. Trotsky failed to attend the funeral six day's later – seen in some quarters as evidence of the distance between the two men in contrast to the close relationship between Lenin and Stalin. Recent research indicates 'no persuasive evidence' that Stalin actually plotted to keep Trotsky away from the funeral.

January 1925

Trotsky was forced out of his post as narkom of defence. Later that year Trotsky published his collected writings. These were interpreted as further evidence of earlier divisions between Trotsky and Lenin.

April 1925

At the Fourteenth Party Conference, Stalin's policy of 'Socialism in One Country' was formally adopted, signalling a complete rejection of Trotsky's ideas of 'permanent revolution' which envisaged Bolshevik involvement in working-class struggle throughout Europe, not just in Russia.

October 1926

Trotsky was expelled from the Politburo.

October 1927

At the Fifteeth Party Congress, Trotsky had to resort to using an underground press to print his programme. When Trotsky spoke to the Central Committee he was heckled throughout his speech.

7 November 1927

Trotsky mounted his final demonstrations against his opponents in Moscow and Leningrad, but was subjected to abuse.

14 November 1927

Trotsky and Zinoviev were expelled from the party and Trotsky was evicted from his flat in the Kremlin.

January 1928

Trotsky was formally banished to the provinces.

1929

Trotsky was exiled to Turkey.

Trotsky as Commissar for War, 1921.

Challenging History Resource Pack. Text © John Traynor; Illustrations © Thomas Nelson & Sons Ltd; Photographs © as listed on p.2, sourced texts on p.44. Published by Thomas Nelson & Sons Ltd 1999.

STALIN

July 1917

Unlike Trotsky, Stalin had been born in acute poverty. As an old Bolshevik he had paid his dues within the party, not least with his sustained periods of exile in the pre-Revolutionary period. In the early summer of 1917 he was released from jail by the Provisional Government. With Lenin in hiding and several leading Bolsheviks in jail, Stalin and his rival Sverdlov now occupied key positions in the party.

Stalin played an important role in the Party Congress held in Petrograd between 26 July and 31 August, and now became a member of the new Central Committee.

August to October 1917

Stalin was busy writing and editing articles for the Bolshevik Military Organisation. Stalin was distinctly unhappy with Trotsky's appointment as Chairman of the Central Executive Committee.

October 1917

Although it remains the case that Stalin did not play an heroic part in the Bolshevik uprising, recent research suggests that Stalin's role was more central than previously thought. Stalin was asked to update his colleagues on the progress of the struggle, and analysis of his speech reveals that Stalin was kept informed of details of all aspects of the uprising. When Lenin came to power Stalin was made a member of the cabinet of the new government – Sovnarkom. Stalin regularly attended the meetings of this key body, although his absences from Moscow on Civil War duties from 1918 onwards meant this was not always possible. He was also a member of the inner group of Sovnarkom – the 'Little Council'.

Stalin was given the cabinet post of Commissar for Nationalities, possibly because of his Georgian background.

January 1918

Stalin was critical of Trotsky's negotiating stance at the Brest-Litovsk treaty negotiations with Germany. Stalin supported Lenin in his bid to persuade the Party Central Committee to accept German peace terms.

March 1918

Stalin set up his base at the Kremlin in Moscow – he seldom visited Petrograd after the revolution.

April 1918

Stalin served on the commission which drew up the first constitution of the Soviet State.

June 1918

For the next two and a half years Stalin combined his administrative duties with military assignments in the Civil War. As a member of the Council of Labour and Defence, Stalin helped to provide economic support for the armed forces. He repeatedly clashed with Trotsky over the conduct of the war.

August 1918

Following the attempted assassination of Lenin, Stalin demanded 'open, mass, systematic terror'. Stalin served on three separate commissions on aspects of the Cheka (the Bolshevik secret police), although he had no formal responsibility for them, and his knowledge of the inner workings of the Cheka and its secret files was developing substantially.

March 1919

Stalin was appointed to lead the People's Commissariat of State Control. This came about because Stalin had earlier reported to Lenin on the weakness of central leadership over the regional party branches. Stalin's military duties in the Civil War prevented him from working on this project until it was reorganised in February 1920 as the Workers and Peasants Inspectorate (RKI or Rabkrin).

December 1919

The Eighth Party Conference formally established the Organisational Bureau (the Orgburo) and the Political Bureau (the Politburo). The Orgburo dealt with personnel and the assignment of party members to particular jobs. Stalin soon established himself as the most important member of this body.

Summer 1921

Recent research suggests that Stalin's heavy workload and administrative burden took its toll on his health. He may have received treatment for ulcers at this time and appears to have travelled to the North Caucasus for a cure in the summer of 1921. In July 1921, Stalin demanded tougher measures by the party against the Georgian nationalists. Stalin's blunt methods against the Georgians made Lenin aware of how brutal Stalin could be.

Spring 1922

Lenin created the new post of General Secretary of the Communist Party, and on 3 April he appointed Stalin to this post. Historian Orlando Figes writes: 'It was to prove a crucial appointment – one that enabled Stalin to come to power…The key to Stalin's growing power was his control of the party apparatus in the provinces. As the Chairman of the Secretariat, and the only Politburo member in the Orgburo, he could promote his friends and dismiss opponents.'

On 25 April, Stalin gave up his responsibility for the Rabkrin and devoted all of his energy and capacity for political intrigue into deploying his new and extensive powers of patronage. More than 10,000 provincial officials were appointed, mostly with Stalin's approval, in 1922 alone.

May 1922

Lenin suffered a stroke between 25–27 May. During Lenin's period of convalescence his first visitor outside the family was Stalin. Stalin established himself as the main link between Lenin and the Politburo and visited Lenin on a weekly basis in August and September.

Stalin was working to engineer an anti-Trotsky power bloc which has generally been held to have consisted of a triumvirate of himself, Zinoviev and Kamenev. Zinoviev hated Trotsky. Kamenev had been with Stalin in exile in Siberia. Stalin had defended Kamenev when Lenin wanted to expel him from the party after he expressed opposition to the October Revolution. Kamenev was Trotsky's brother-in-law, but was prepared to put family ties to one side to further his own considerable political ambitions. Both felt that they were using Stalin to defeat Trotsky. The reverse was the case. Recent research has suggested that the anti-Trotsky bloc was broader than the triumvirate and actually ran through the whole Politburo, in which Trotsky now found himself completely isolated.

Autumn 1922

Lenin expressed great concern over the heavy-handed manner in which Stalin and his colleague Ordzhonikidze were dealing with the Georgian nationalists.

15 December 1922

Lenin suffered his second major stroke. Stalin took charge of the doctors and issued orders to keep political news from Lenin to prevent the invalid from becoming excited.

However, by Christmas Eve Lenin, who was deeply disturbed by the side of Stalin's character which he had seen during the Georgian affair, had decided to dictate a political testament which included these words on Stalin: 'Comrade Stalin, having become General Secretary has immeasurable power concentrated in his hands, and I am not sure that he always knows how to use that power with sufficient control.'

4 January 1923

Lenin added a postscript to his secret political testament: 'Stalin is too rude, and this fault, entirely acceptable in relations between communists, becomes competely unacceptable in the office of General Secretary…I propose to the comrades that a way be found to remove Stalin from that post and replace him with someone else who differs from Stalin in all respects.'

March 1923

Lenin suffered a further stroke, temporarily depriving him of the power of speech.

December 1923

A two-hour meeting marked the last time Stalin saw Lenin alive.

January 1924

A tumultuous month for Stalin. At Lenin's funeral he made certain that he presented himself as a picture of grief, even though during Lenin's protracted illness he had privately commented that 'he can't even die like a proper leader'.

At the Thirteenth Party Conference in the same month, Stalin told a supportive audience about Trotsky's 'six errors'. This was his first major public attack on Trotsky. Meanwhile Lenin's widow had distributed Lenin's political testament to the senior figures in the party. Fortunately for Stalin, Zinoviev and Kamenev came to his rescue. They were prepared to put Lenin's testament to one side because they knew that Lenin had not been flattering to themselves and they also feared the advantage that a breach could give to Trotsky.

April 1924

Stalin published his work 'Foundations of Leninism'.

November 1925

Stalin published 'Trotskyism or Leninism?', followed the next month by a text in which he criticised Trotsky over the October Revolution.

December 1925

Stalin received 'an ovation from the entire congress'. Significantly Stalin now shifted his attack towards Zinoviev who was now deprived of his political base in Leningrad.

October to November 1926

At the Fifteenth Party Congress, Stalin attacked the 'United Opposition' of Trotsky, Zinoviev and Kamenev.

November 1927

Stalin secured the authority of the Central Committee to demand the expulsion of Trotsky and Zinoviev from the party.

Challenging History Resource Pack. Text © John Traynor; Illustrations © Thomas Nelson & Sons Ltd; Photographs © as listed on p.2, sourced texts on p.44. Published by Thomas Nelson & Sons Ltd 1999.

Recent interpretations of Stalin's rise to power

Source A

He had no illusions about the calibre of his rivals. Trotsky was a windbag, Zinoviev a weakling and Kamenev a moderate to be out manoeuvred at will. No member of the Politburo had the qualities necessary to squash him, and he could always win a voting majority by balancing his alliances. True, the Central Committee was not quite under his control, but it already contained his closest associates…As for the rank and file, this now underwent a transformation which put it firmly behind Stalin. To commemorate Lenin's death, the Party admitted 200,000 new members…of course, the newcomers were carefully sifted by Stalin's machine…The chief victims of the purges would be Old Bolsheviks and those joining the party before 1924. They would be replaced by these latecomers, ignorant, unsophisticated and avid readers of Stalin, who had never seen Lenin, or more importantly, Trotsky in full cry.

Alex de Jonge, *Stalin and the Shaping of the Soviet Union* (1986)

Source B

Above all, Stalin's rise as an effective administrator depended on his capacity for work, unrelenting and immensely varied. Here was a man, perhaps the only one at Lenin's disposal, who could take on almost any kind of job, whether or not he had any background in the matter at hand, learn enough about it to make definite decisions under severe pressure of time and deal with the most pressing problems…The years 1918–22 are matchless education for Stalin in the direction of the new Russian empire…almost always under emergency conditions.

Robert H. McNeal, *Stalin: Man and Ruler* (1988)

Source C

That the [Bolshevik] regime survived owes much to people like Stalin, in whom previously untapped qualities were discovered, most especially an aptitude for exercising power. Stalin's affinity for authority began with a zest for it. This sounds obvious enough, but there are serious grounds to doubt that many of the leading Bolsheviks, Trotsky, Zinoviev and Bukharin among them, fully shared this quality. Certainly none of them displayed in the five years of Lenin's rule the capacity for politics and administration that Stalin revealed in this time.

Robert H. McNeal, *Stalin: Man and Ruler* (1988)

Source D

In 1922…Lenin called Stalin 'a person of authority'. On what did this aura of authority rest? Not on an heroic image. Stalin was not a highly visible hero of the revolution and civil war in these years. The fame of Trotsky, the organiser of the Red Army and eloquent speaker and writer, was far greater, and a number of others – such as Zinoviev, Kamenev and Bukharin – probably received more attention in the Soviet media than did Stalin.

Robert H. McNeal, *Stalin: Man and Ruler* (1988)

TASKS

These two exercises will enable you to consider:

- the factors which enabled Stalin to win the power struggle;

- the factors which made Trotsky unable to win the power struggle.

1   Work in groups of three or four people. Look at the list of fifteen factors involved in the rise to power of Stalin.

   - Each member of your group has to select two factors which they think are of decisive importance and write them down (without telling the rest of the group their selection).

   - In turn, each person has to say the first factor they selected and justify their choice.

   - Repeat the process with the second factor.

   - As a group, look at all of the factors and agree an order of importance **for the whole group**.

   - Each group should then report back to see if any consensus emerges.

2   Repeat this process with regard to Trotsky.

Challenging History Resource Pack. Text © John Traynor; Illustrations © Thomas Nelson & Sons Ltd; Photographs © as listed on p.2, sourced texts on p.44. Published by Thomas Nelson & Sons Ltd 1999.

Factors which enabled Stalin to win the power struggle

❶ As General Secretary of the Communist Party, Stalin was better placed than anyone to build up a power base inside the party. The party was seen by Stalin as the means of achieving power.

❷ Stalin was able to conceal his true feelings for Lenin and presented himself as a devoted follower and the true disciple of Lenin.

❸ The other members of the Politburo were never able to present a united front against Stalin.

❹ Stalin was seriously underestimated by the other Bolsheviks.

❺ Stalin 'did not confide his innermost thoughts to anybody.'

❻ Stalin had an utterly ruthless personality which equipped him perfectly for a power struggle. Stalin's single-mindedness meant that he devoted all his waking hours to thinking how to manipulate the situation.

❼ The other Bolsheviks tended to have a middle class, intellectual background. In contrast, Stalin's upbringing was exceptionally harsh. This made him a tougher character than his rivals.

❽ The nature of Lenin's illness meant that he was never able to effectively convey his deep concerns about Stalin to the Bolshevik elite or to the Russian people.

❾ In May 1924, Kamenev and Zinoviev came to Stalin's rescue when they defused criticisms made by Lenin of Stalin in his political testament.

❿ Stalin was more in tune with what the Communist Party itself wanted in the period after Lenin.

⓫ Stalin roused the 1926 Party Conference with his slogan of 'Socialism in One Country'. This gave him a broader appeal than Trotsky with his concept of 'Permanent Revolution'.

⓬ Trotsky failed to attend Lenin's funeral and fell ill at a key point in the struggle.

⓭ Trotsky, Zinoviev and Bukharin were all much better communicators than Stalin when it came to both speaking and writing. However, the struggle took place behind the scenes rather than on the national stage.

⓮ Stalin was an expert at concealing his ambition. On several occasions he shook hands with Trotsky at Politburo meetings whereas other figures did not conceal their hatred of Trotsky.

⓯ Stalin was able to convince the party that he stood for unity while the other candidates were a threat to the party's cohesion.

THE APPEAL OF THE NAZI PARTY:

Preview

The failure of the Munich Beer-Hall Putsch taught Hitler a profound lesson about the difficulties of direct confrontation with the power of the state. He came out of prison in December 1924 knowing that the prospect of a successful armed seizure of power was completely unrealistic. Hitler made it clear in *Mein Kampf* that the strategy employed by the NSDAP would, from now on, concentrate on the ballot box and the drive for seats in the Reichstag (the German Parliament).

Between 1924–28 the Nazi structure was re-organised, rallies became more elaborate, Hitler's authority was consolidated, and a challenge to his authority in 1926 was brushed aside. Despite these organisational changes, the Reichstag elections of May 1928 – in which the Nazis gained only 2.6 per cent of the votes – showed that on the national stage, Hitler remained a figure of only marginal consequence. As Richard Overy puts it: 'Until 1928 Nazism was an insignificant political force trying to win factory workers away from Marxism…It was a marginal political movement on the radical right.'

All historians agree that the turning point in the fortunes of the Nazis came about not through a Hitler speech, or a Goebbels' rally, but thousands of miles away in the frenzied selling of stocks and shares in the Wall Street Crash of October 1929. In the words of William Carr: 'It is inconceivable that Hitler could ever have come to power had not the Weimar Republic been subjected to the unprecedented strain of a world economic crisis.' As Laurence Rees explains in *The Nazis: A Warning From History*: 'Shortly after the election, (of 1928) the economic and political situation in Germany radically changed. First an agricultural depression hit home and then the Wall Street Crash triggered the most serious economic crisis ever encountered in Germany, as the United States called in its loans.'

Although the depression which followed the Wall Street Crash devastated the German economy, there was no guarantee that the German people would now turn to Hitler. How was the party able to extend its appeal beyond the fringes of extreme right-wing activity (where it appeared to be marooned as late as the Reichstag elections of May 1928) into the mainstream of German politics as shown in the Reichstag elections of September 1930? We will now examine some of the most recent findings in this area.

Who voted for Hitler? Recent interpretations

Until very recently it seemed unlikely that this element of Hitler's rise to power would be subject to major historical revision. A substantial amount of initial research combined with local studies to provide what appeared to be a fairly clear-cut picture of who voted for Hitler and who did not.

This position is summarised in the table alongside.

Who supported the National Socialists? (traditional interpretation)

- The middle class (Mittelstand) and the lower middle class. Typically these groups included small businessmen, shopkeepers and artisans (tradesmen and craftsmen).
- Heartland support in small towns and villages.
- Large support in the most rural areas, particularly from small landowners and fishermen.

Note: the 'classic' Nazi voter was likely to be young, male and Protestant.

Which groups were resistant to the National Socialists? (traditional interpretation)

- The working class.
- Catholics, females and industrial workers.

Note: resistance to the Nazis was greatest in the largest cities and towns.

Scene from block of flats showing use of swastikas and hammer and sickle.

New interpretations

It should be stressed that it is not our intention here to discard all elements of this picture and present something completely new to take its place. Rather, the point is to suggest significant modifications in the light of recent research. This suggests that at the height of its electoral appeal in the summer of 1932, the National Socialist Party was a much more broadly based political movement than has previously been acknowledged. The NSDAP is now seen by many experts as more than just a magnet to the middle and particularly lower middle classes. It is now claimed that the party is more accurately seen as the most socially homogenous party in German electoral history in the whole period from 1871–1933. This enabled the Nazis to lay claim to be the Volkspartei (People's Party) – a claim which its rivals could never make.

The new consensus is that by 1932 the party was drawing on an unprecedentedly broad social spectrum of support among Protestant (but not Catholic) voters, including some workers and members of the professional and commercial elites, as well as members of the middle and lower-middle classes.

The working class Workers were not proportionately represented in the membership or the leadership of the Nazi party, although there was a left-wing faction represented by Gregor Strasser which hoped to attract support from the urban and industrial areas.

However, if the definition of working class is extended beyond manual workers to include occupations such as shop assistants, clerks and tradesmen, then Nazi support in this area appears much more significant. It is more accurate to say that it was the organised working class, such as trade union members and workers with links to the Social Democratic Party of Germany (SPD) or the German Communist Party (KPD), who remained resistant to the National Socialists.

Women were not traditionally regarded as natural Nazi supporters. Before 1930 the party was appealing to more male voters than female. However, after 1930 the party gained a greater proportion of female voters. In the Reichstag elections of March 1933, more women than men were voting Nazi.

Elite groups Recent research into electoral results in the larger cities shows that significant numbers in the wealthier suburbs tended to support Hitler. Wealthy businessmen, professional and high-ranking civil servants can be included in this grouping.

Scene from Hitler rally in 1933.

Challenging History Resource Pack. Text © John Traynor; Illustrations © Thomas Nelson & Sons Ltd; Photographs © as listed on p.2, sourced texts on p.44. Published by Thomas Nelson & Sons Ltd 1999.

The views of historians

Source A

Hitler's propaganda techniques for winning the masses could achieve little success, however, without the external conditions which exposed an electoral market to the Nazi political alternative. Without the Depression, the worsening crisis of government and state, and the disintegration of the bourgeois liberal-conservative parties, this mass 'market' would not have become available and Hitler would have continued to have been an insignificant minority taste on the lunatic fringes of the political system. Even in the Depression… the 'masses' were won to Nazism usually by more prosaic routes than being swept off their feet at a Hitler rally. For the most part Hitler was preaching to the converted or half-converted in such rallies. Among the non-committed…the impact was often far from charismatic…

Ian Kershaw, *Hitler: Profiles in Power* (1991)

Source B

The winning of the support of a third of the voting population between 1929 and 1932 was an extraordinary achievement of political mobilisation… With the party propaganda machine centralised in the hands of Goebbels since April 1930, the image was shaped with increasing skill and direction. Campaign slogans, themes, speakers and publicity were centrally orchestrated, but with attention to local or regional emphases. New, striking techniques were deployed, as in the second presidential campaign in spring 1932 when an aeroplane was chartered to carry Hitler to his election rallies under the slogan 'the Fuhrer over Germany.' The image was suggestive of a modern, technological world, though one in which true German values would be restored and would dominate. Above all, the image that Nazi propaganda ceaselessly portrayed was that of power, strength, dynamism and youth'.

Ian Kershaw, *Hitler: Profiles in Power* (1991)

Source C

The supporters who made the NSDAP the largest membership and electoral party in Germany by mid-1932 were animated less by the extreme histrionics of the party's leadership than by calculations of political rationality similar to those that prompted the choices of other voters or political activists.

Jane Caplan, 'The Rise of National Socialism' from
Modern Germany Reconsidered 1870–1945,
edited by Gordon Martel (1992)

TASKS

1 Work in groups of three or four people.

   (a) Produce a presentation showing a traditional interpretation of who supported Hitler. Use your textbooks to produce statistical charts and tables summarising the elections of 1928–33. Emphasise the performance of the Nazi Party and the groups which were seen as central to the support of the party. You will also want to emphasise regional variations.

   (b) Repeat **(a)**, but this time show how historians have modified their views in this area.

2 'From fringe movement to the largest party in German history' – to what extent was the rapid improvement in the fortunes of the Nazi Party due to the charismatic leadership of Adolf Hitler?

3 **Essay** Who voted for the Nazis?

Preview

> *'Every day the largest country in the world woke up with his name on its lips. All day long that name rang out in the voices of actors, resounded in song, stared out from the pages of every newspaper. That name was conferred, as the highest of honours, on factories, collective farms, streets and towns. During the most terrible of all wars, soldiers went to their deaths intoning his name. During that war the city of Stalingrad bled almost to death…but the city that bore his name was not surrendered to the enemy. During the political trials organised by him, his victims glorified his name as they died. Even in the camps, his portrait looked down on millions of people, who corralled behind barbed wire at his behest…raised cities beyond the Arctic Circle, and perished in their hundreds of thousands. Statues of this man in granite and bronze towered over the immense country.'*
>
> Edvard Radzinsky, *Stalin* (1996)

As Edvard Radzinsky makes clear in the beginning of his compelling recent biography of Stalin, few politicians have had such a wide-ranging impact on the country they have led. It has generally been assumed that Stalin's control of the Soviet Union between 1928–39 was absolute and that in this period no views contrary to those of Stalin were ever expressed. It seems reasonable to conclude that a major shift from this position is unlikely.

An abundance of evidence from people who lived through the Stalinist era provides support for this perspective. For example, in 1936 Kornei Chukovsky, a popular children's writer, returned from a meeting with Stalin and wrote in his private journal: 'Something extraordinary had happened to the audience! I looked round…every face was full of love and tenderness, inspired…For all of us, to see him, simply to see him, made us all happy…We reacted to every movement of his with reverence. I had never supposed myself capable of such feelings.'

Another writer recalled: 'Stalin was like God for us. We just believed he was an absolutely perfect individual, and he lived somewhere in the Kremlin, a light always in his window, and he was thinking about us, about each of us.' It is interesting to note that both of these sources, and there are thousands more like them, were written without direct coercion.

However, the recent opening up of hitherto secret archives has at least enabled historians to develop a more sophisticated picture of Stalin's rule. Evidence of disquiet at the extreme nature of Stalin's policies and signs of a degree of opposition to Stalin have now begun to emerge. In addition the image of the NKVD (Stalin's secret police) as a supremely effective, ruthlessly efficient organisation has also been called into question. Our purpose in this unit then is to look at the views of historians who have recently researched this period and so to examine the extent of Stalin's control of the Soviet Union between 1928–39.

On 1 January 1937, more than 40,000 young athletes paraded through Red Square.

Challenging History Resource Pack. Text © John Traynor; Illustrations © Thomas Nelson & Sons Ltd; Photographs © as listed on p.2, sourced texts on p.44. Published by Thomas Nelson & Sons Ltd 1999.

The views of historians

Source A

By 1932, a number of senior figures in the party and leadership were growing extremely anxious about Stalin's policies and methods. Since collectivisation, and amidst the excesses of industrialisation, a number of informal groups had met to discuss how to restrain or remove General Secretary Stalin. The most important was led by Martemyan Ryutin, who circulated clandestinely a two-hundred page attack, fifty pages of which were devoted to Stalin's own personality...Ryutin and his supporters wanted Stalin removed, democracy within the party, slower industrialisation and an end to formal collectivisation.

Jonathan Lewis and Phillip Whitehead,
Stalin: A Time for Judgement (1989)

Source B

It remains that Kirov was Stalin's principal potential rival. Aged forty-eight at the time of his death, Kirov was seven years younger than Stalin. In almost ten years as party chief of Leningrad Province he had become a well-established national figure. If he wanted a turn at the top, he could not afford to wait for Stalin to die, but perhaps his relative youth might recommend itself to a number of party activists. He was good-looking and a powerful speaker. Most important, he was a Great Russian...the Soviet State remained Russian at its core. The appearance of...a Georgian like Stalin at the top of the movement was an anomaly of the revolution.

Robert H. McNeal, *Stalin: Man and Ruler* (1988)

Source C

The great majority of the population woke up happily to the relentless blare of the loudspeakers, sped eagerly to work, participated enthusiastically in the daily public meetings at which their enemies were anathematised, and read skimpy newspaper reports of the trials which showed how very reliable the secret police were...The public trials, with their magnificent ritual of retribution, were one of the distractions from everyday life.

Edvard Radzinsky, *Stalin* (1996)

Source D

There is no point in trying to rehabilitate Stalin. The established impression that he slaughtered, tortured, imprisoned and oppressed on a grand scale is not in error. On the other hand, it is impossible to understand this immensely gifted politician by attributing solely to him all the crimes and suffering of his era, or to conceive him simply as a monster and a mental case. From youth until death he was a fighter in what he, and many others, regarded as a just war...The class war...Stalin rose to eminence among people who subscribed to this outlook, not only party activists but many members of Russia's vast underclass, urban or rural. They were ready for bloodshed.

Robert H. McNeal, *Stalin: Man and Ruler* (1988)

Source E

Both Western and Stalinist writers have been interested in showing that the Soviet bureaucracy was grimly efficient: totalitarian to Western writers, monolithic or solidly united to Stalinists. The near consensus on a monolithic apparatus has made it easy to overlook evidence and to believe that an untrained and uneducated bureaucracy in a huge, developing peasant country somehow functioned and obeyed well enough to be termed totalitarian...this study questions the applicability of the totalitarian model...Recent specialised historical studies of the period after 1929 have shown that policy making in the early Stalin years was sometimes unstructured and erratic...None of these works have suggested that Stalin was not the most powerful political actor, but some of them have implied that he was not necessarily the author of every initiative.

J. Arch Getty, *Origins of the Great Purges* (1985)

Source F

In just a few years he decimated the Russian peasantry and built on its bones Europe's biggest war machine, rivalling that of Nazi Germany. He then viciously destroyed the commanding core of his army, interfered with the development and production of war technologies, and massacred, in a frenzy of political and social "cleansing", millions of loyal supporters, skilful professionals and workers.

Vladislav Zubok and Constantine Pleshakov,
Inside the Kremlin's Cold War (1996)

Key points in the development of Stalin's dictatorship

1927 – November
Trotsky expelled from the Communist Party.

1928 – May
Miners in the Shakhty region put on trial for sabotage.

1929 – December
Stalin's 50th birthday greeted with first signs of a personality cult.

1930 – March
Stalin publishes 'Dizzy with Success' advocating slowing down of collectivisation programme.

1931 – January
Stalin gives orders for rapid development of Magnitogorsk industrial complex.

1932 – May
Stalin calls together literary figures and advocates the notion of 'socialist realism'.

1933 – May
New wave of material celebrating Stalin's greatness.

1934 – December
Assassination of his closest rival, Kirov.

1935 – January
Zinoviev and Kamenev convicted of indirect involvement in the murder of Kirov.

1936 – August
Public 'show' trial of Zinoviev, Kamenev and others followed by appointment of Yezhov as Head of Police; and intensification of terror. Yezhov tells the NKVD that 'when you cut down the forest, wood chips fly'. By now, internal passports are mandatory and under the Criminal Code virtually anything can be interpreted as a criminal action.

1937 – June
Secret trial of Tukhachevsky and other senior military personnel.

1938 – March
Public trial of Bukharin and others, followed later in the year by the replacement of Yezhov by Beria as Head of Police.

1939 – March
Stalin tells the Eighteenth Party Congress that the mass purges are over.

Elements of resistance to Stalin's rule, 1929–34

1929 – January
Stalin attempts to secure condemnation of Bukharin from a commission of the Politburo and the Presidium of Central Control Commission. Despite the presence on the committee of a number of Stalinists, it fails to provide the vote of censure which Stalin wants.

1932
Stalin's wife, Nadezhda Allilueva, commits suicide after a series of bitter arguments. She had told Stalin that she disagreed with his collectivisation policy and with his cruelty towards party members.

In the same year Martemyan Ryutin circulates a document criticising Stalin's leadership and personality. Ryutin is subsequently arrested, but Stalin's demand for the death penalty is overturned and Ryutin is merely expelled from the party.

1934
At the Seventeenth Party Congress, Kirov is approached by a faction within the party which, recalling the spirit of Lenin's testament, wants to replace Stalin with someone more tolerant and move Stalin to a lesser post. Historian Roy Medvedev claims that in a secret ballot 270 delegates voted against Stalin, giving him an insight into the extent of his unpopularity. However, before the year is over, Kirov is dead. The Great Terror is about to begin. Open criticism of Stalin is now consigned to the past.

TASKS

1 Historians have tended to be in agreement as to the nature of life in Stalin's Soviet Union. Explain in your own words what this verdict has been and why there has been little scope for disagreement.

2 What elements of the picture have now been changed or modified?

3 How substantial are these changes? Do you feel that the view of Stalin's Soviet Union has not really been altered by the new research, or would you argue that it has now changed?

4 How serious were the difficulties faced by Stalin between 1932–34? How did he overcome them?

5 To what extent are the historians whose views are presented here in agreement about the nature of Stalin's rule?

Challenging History Resource Pack. Text © John Traynor; Illustrations © Thomas Nelson & Sons Ltd; Photographs © as listed on p.2, sourced texts on p.44. Published by Thomas Nelson & Sons Ltd 1999.

Stalin at the Soviet Congress in December 1936.

Preview

The description of Nazi Germany as a totalitarian state was first advocated by historians such as Hannah Arendt and Karl Dietrich Bracher, writing in the 1950s and 1960s. Since then, many historians have been happy to follow this model. Central ingredients of this model have been the authority of a fanatical and charismatic leader, the unquestioning loyalty of a monolithic, cohesive party, the systematic use of terror and the oppression of the masses through a highly-efficient secret police (the Gestapo). Put simply, the central assumption has been that people accepted the National Socialist regime because they had no choice.

It would be wrong to ignore the fact that Hitler systematically set about destroying many of the key elements of a democratic system.

Chronology of constraints

1933

27 February

Reichstag fire, immediately followed by claims that this heralds an attempted communist uprising.

28 February

Decree 'For the Protection of People and State' sees the suspension of civil rights and wholesale arrests of communists and other socialist opponents.

20 March

Dachau concentration camp opens.

23 March

Reichstag passes an Enabling Act giving Hitler sweeping powers.

2 May

Trade unions are dissolved and replaced by single German Labour Front (DAF).

10 May

The works of 'un-German' authors are thrown on bonfires across the country.

22 June

SPD is banned.

14 July

Prohibition of all political parties apart from the Nazi Party.

1934

30 January

The sovereignty of the Lander (or federal states) is taken away under the Law on the Reconstruction of the Reich.

24 April

Creation of the People's Court, led by Roland Freisler, to deal with treasonable offences.

30 June

'Night of the Long Knives' purge against the SA culminates in the execution of Ernst Rohm and the extinction of the SA as a political force.

While we must continue to bear in mind the dictatorial nature of Hitler's regime, we must now also be aware that repressive measures were directed against the weaker and less popular sections of society and not towards the population in general.

This was a regime which worked very hard to secure and retain support from ordinary German people. Hitler was acutely aware of the fragility of his own popularity and was extremely wary of doing anything to jeopardise his public standing. From the moment Hitler became Chancellor, the Nazis carried out a number of actions which enabled the regime to be depicted in a positive light.

Challenging History Resource Pack. Text © John Traynor; Illustrations © Thomas Nelson & Sons Ltd; Photographs © as listed on p.2, sourced texts on p.44. Published by Thomas Nelson & Sons Ltd 1999.

- First of all, it is essential to recall that in many respects Hitler did not have a difficult act to follow. In the last, desperate years of the Weimar Republic a once proud nation had been racked by poverty, unemployment and food shortages. A country which prided itself on its sense of order now witnessed bitter street fighting and political chaos. Above all, many Germans feared the spectre of revolutionary Marxism. Hitler promised bread for the masses, a reduction in unemployment, the restoration of law and order, the suppression of Marxism, a return to traditional values and the moral regeneration of the nation. Hitler's task was made easier by the fact that many people tended to use the final years of the Weimar period as a reference point, rather than the relatively prosperous period of 1924–28. This made it possible for the Nazis to build up the image of an 'economic miracle'.

- Many Germans saw Hitler as a moderate figure, opposing extremists in the Communist Party but also restraining extremists within his own party. The research of Ian Kershaw and other historians into popular opinion has shown that the Fuhrer's image was remarkably popular and durable throughout the period.

- The Nazis claimed that they were establishing a classless Volksgemeinschaft (People's Community). Nazi posters and speeches spoke of 'Ein Reich, Ein Volk, Ein Fuhrer' (One Country, One People, One Leader).

- The 'Winter help' programme involved wealthier people collecting money and making donations to provide food and aid for the unemployed.

- The 'one pot meal' was aimed at families who could make do with simpler meals once a week and donate the money saved to the poor.

- The Strength Through Joy (Kraft durch freude KDF) Movement provided sports clubs and subsidised holidays for workers.

- Workers were subjected to a concerted propaganda campaign. The Nazis played heavily on the symbolism of phrases such as 'German quality work', 'the honour of labour', ' a factory community' (Werksgemeinschaft) and 'a national community'. This was developed further through the 'Beauty of Labour' programme.

- DAF replaced the 'class conflict' of the trade unions with a 'movement' celebrating 'the dignity of labour'. The leader of the DAF, Robert Ley, repeatedly stated, 'I gave my hand to the men'. This constituted 'support' to workers who felt 'betrayed' and 'sold out' by the weak government and exploitative business practices of the Weimar period.

- Hitler stressed that 'there is no dishonour in menial labour', criticised 'intellectuals' and praised the virtue of farmers, workers and peasants.

- The rearmament programme boosted the economy, reduced unemployment and provided new areas of war production (e.g. Bremen and the aircraft industry, Salzgitter with the Herman Goering Reichswerke).

- There was a general increase in wages (although this was achieved by working longer hours).

- The German historian Detlev Peukert has shown that there was widespread appreciation of the imposition of law and order (bicycles could be left unattended, 'loafers' were made to work).

- Projects such as the construction of a national autobahn system, the production of the Volkswagen car and the production of cheap transistor radios provided employment and made the regime look dynamic, efficient and progressive.

- Foreign policy successes between 1935–38 further boosted the prestige of Hitler.

The perfect propaganda image: a child presents flowers to Hitler (1938).

Challenging History Resource Pack. Text © John Traynor; Illustrations © Thomas Nelson & Sons Ltd; Photographs © as listed on p.2, sourced texts on p.44. Published by Thomas Nelson & Sons Ltd 1999.

Resistance to Hitler

20 July 1944

The Fuhrer's command centre – the Wolf's Lair – had been breached. Its isolated position in a forest clearing near the East Prussian town of Rastenburg was no defence because the assassin was more than familiar with the surroundings. The massive security which surrounded the Fuhrer could not contend with the fact that the man who had decided to take Hitler's life had his own security pass. In any case the face of the handsome, highly-decorated general was well known to the guards. As a result, Claus von Stauffenberg was able to enter the innermost security zone, known as the Fuhrer Restricted Area, without arousing suspicion.

The war briefing had already begun and Stauffenberg was late. He would rush into the Fuhrer's Headquarters offering apologies for his delay. The case which he clutched contained two pounds of high explosive. He was unable to get as close to Hitler as he would have liked but Stauffenberg did not have much time. After placing his case on the far side of the table he withdrew, muttering quietly as he left, as if he had something urgent to deal with. Within minutes of leaving the building the blast went off. The wooden barracks were completely destroyed. The wreckage was lifted high into the air. Stauffenberg looked back at the shattered barracks and concluded that Hitler was dead. In the confusion he was able to leave the base and take a flight to Berlin. By the time he arrived there it had emerged that Hitler had suffered burns and minor injuries but he had not been seriously wounded.

The July Plot had failed and Stauffenberg and his supporters were doomed. Stauffenberg was arrested within hours and was executed on the night of 20–21 July. The most well-known episode in the German resistance to Hitler had come close to success but was unable to dislodge Hitler. The attention which the July Plot has received has tended to obscure the fact that there were no less than fifteen attempts to kill Hitler and that a wide variety of Germans offered, in their different ways, resistance to Hitler. Here we will examine some of the less well-known elements of the resistance.

The Wolf's Lair in Rastenberg

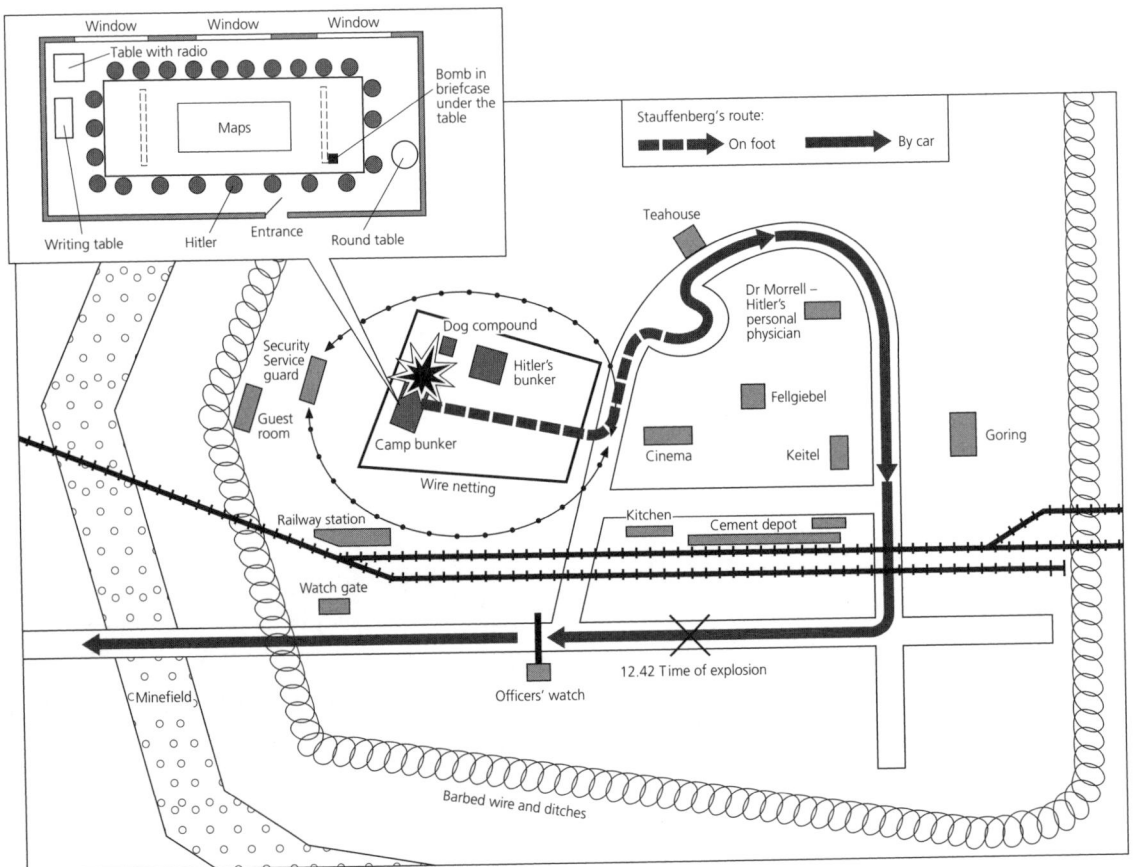

Some of the individuals who resisted Hitler

Johan George Elser	During the 1920s Elser supported the German Communist Party and was a member of the League of Red Front-line Fighters. During the crisis over Czechoslovakia in 1938 Elser decided to carry out an assassination attempt against Hitler. He placed a timed explosive device at the Burgerbrau beer hall in Munich. It exploded on 8 November 1939 and eight people were killed, but Hitler had left the room a few minutes earlier. Elser was arrested on the same day and after spells in Sachsenhausen and Dachau concentration camps, he was murdered on 9 April 1945.
Hans and Sophie Scholl	Following the outbreak of war, two students at Munich University set up the White Rose resistance group. They openly distributed leaflets condemning the treatment of the Jews and urging German youth to 'rise up' against the brutality of Nazi rule. They were arrested and executed in February 1943. On the day of the execution, students at their university demonstrated their loyalty to Hitler.
'Beppo' Romer	Romer, a former leader of the Freikorp, brought together revolutionary militants from the left and right wing of the Weimar period. Between 1942–43 nearly 150 members of his group were tried and executed by the People's Court.
Count Helmuth James von Moltke	A member of the legal profession, he practised law in Berlin in the pre-war years. When war broke out he served in the Supreme Command of the Armed Forces but he was already deeply opposed to the Nazi regime. From 1940 he began to convene secret meetings of opponents at his Kreisau estate in Silesia. Moltke established links with other resistance groups but this culminated in his arrest on 9 January 1944. He was found guilty by the People's Court and executed in Plotzensee prison on 23 January 1945.
Dietrich Bonhoeffer	Bonhoeffer was a Protestant theologian and Doctor of Philosophy. His support for religious tolerance and his deep personal convictions led, in 1940, to him being banned from lecturing and publishing. This pushed him from religious to political resistance. He became a representative of the German Resistance Movement but was arrested by the Gestapo on 5 April 1943. Following a period at Buchenwald concentration camp he was eventually murdered in Flossenburg on 9 April 1945.

Resisting the Nazis: some of the groups who opposed Hitler, 1933–45

Name of group	Composition and purpose	Dates of activity	Fate
The Kreisau Circle	Created by Count Helmuth James von Moltke. The group had a Christian and Socialist philosophy.	Secret meetings at Moltke's Kreisau estate began in 1940.	Moltke was arrested in 1944 and executed in 1945.
Swing groups	Young people whose main interest was American 'swing music'. The movement spread across dance halls. The passion was music but the deliberately casual lifestyle represented a form of low-level resistance to the Nazi culture.	Emerged towards the end of the 1930s and continued into the war.	Like the Eidelweiss Pirates, Gestapo reports on 'decadent youth' continued into the war years, suggesting that a substantial section of German youth were not prepared to be regimented.
Eidelweiss Pirates	Young people in urban areas, mainly teenagers, wearing eidelweiss badges (a small, white alpine plant) and distinctive clothes. They presented a radical alternative for young people alienated by the regimented nature of the Hitler Youth.	These groups developed on a localised basis in several cities in Western Germany in the late 1930s.	The groups became more widespread during the war years and attracted adverse comment from Hitler Youth groups. Some of the ring leaders were arrested and imprisoned, but historians agree that the Nazis were unable to destroy this aspect of youth culture. Several thousand youths took part across Germany.
The Red Orchestra	A left-wing opposition movement set up by a young Luftwaffe pilot named Harro Schulze-Boysen. He joined forces with Arvid and Mildred Harnach. The organisation was given its name – Rote Kapelle – by the Gestapo.	In 1932 Boysen became a member of the Young German Order, but his journal was banned in April 1933 and he was arrested. When he was released he became a key member of the Red Orchestra. During the war he passed information to the Russians.	Boysen and other members of the Red Orchestra were arrested in 1942. He was executed on 22 December 1942, along with his wife, Libertas.
Military opposition	Diverse groups within the military actually constituted the most serious threat to Hitler. A conservative group formed around Carl Goerdeler (the former Mayor of Leipzig) and Ludwig Beck who was the army Chief of Staff until his resignation in 1938.	This group stemmed from the conservative elite who had originally supported Hitler, but who became increasingly concerned with his foreign and racial policies. Goerdeler was chosen by the civilian-military resistance to be the future Chancellor if Hitler could be removed.	Following the abortive July Plot, Goerdeler was arrested on 12 August 1944 after a search lasting several weeks. He was sentenced to death in September and executed on 2 February 1945.

TASKS

Essays

1   What evidence is there to suggest that Hitler was a popular leader of Germany after he became Chancellor in January 1933?

2   What was more important in sustaining Hitler's personal power: the policies of the leadership or the use of terror?

3   To what extent did the Nazis succeed in eliminating opposition to Hitler?

Challenging History Resource Pack. Text © John Traynor; Illustrations © Thomas Nelson & Sons Ltd; Photographs © as listed on p.2, sourced texts on p.44. Published by Thomas Nelson & Sons Ltd 1999.

Preview

Historians are in no doubt as to the extent of Hitler's anti-Semitism. However, they do not necessarily agree about the nature of his leadership in this area of government policy in the period from 1933 onwards. Did Hitler come to power with firm ideas and clear intentions, or with violent impulses but no clearly developed plans?

Some historians have placed Hitler at the very centre of anti-Semitic policy in the Third Reich. They argue that Hitler set the tone, dictated the timing and approved the finer detail of the systematic campaign against the Jews which was launched in 1933 and culminated in the Holocaust, which took place against the background of Hitler's racial war against Poland and the Soviet Union.

Other historians take a rather different view. They agree that Hitler was violently anti-Semitic and they do not intend to lessen to any degree Hitler's ultimate moral responsibility for the Holocaust. However, they portray Hitler as an indecisive character, having to contend with

A Berlin department store suspected of being in Jewish ownership.

virulent anti-Semites within his own party, whilst concentrating as Chancellor on the primary responsibility of reducing unemployment and restoring economic prosperity. They contend that Hitler did not have a clear idea of how to resolve the 'Jewish Question' and argue that the 'Final Solution' was only arrived at after a series of other avenues had been explored. They see the road to the extermination camps as a twisted path rather than a straight line.

In the first part of this unit we will examine the year 1933 in detail. You can then decide which interpretation of Hitler, at least in his first year in office, is closest to the truth.

1933: a case study

30 January

Although there is no immediate panic, within weeks of Hitler becoming Chancellor a number of Jewish artists and intellectuals take the decision to leave Germany. The scientist Albert Einstein who is visiting the USA at the time decides never to return to Germany. At this time there are approximately 525,000 Jews in Germany. They are fully integrated into German society and play a full role in cultural, scientific, economic and sporting life. Within six years a century of equal opportunities and integration will be eliminated. By 1939 the Nazis will have enacted more than 400 laws designed to isolate and humiliate German Jews. Other groups subjected to persecution will include the Gypsies (Roma), political dissidents, homosexuals, the handicapped and Jehovah's Witnesses.

March

A series of violent anti-Jewish incidents occur across the country in the wake of the March elections. Many of these initiatives appear to stem from the radical elements within the Nazi movement. The SA seize dozens of Jews in Berlin and they are taken to concentration camps. In Breslau, Jewish lawyers and judges are beaten. In Bavaria a Jewish man is taken from his house and killed. Other initiatives are more bureaucratic. In Cologne, Jews are banned from using municipal sports facilities. Hitler offers no public comment. The interpretation of many Germans is that Hitler is trying to hold back many of the extremists within his own party.

Challenging History Resource Pack. Text © John Traynor; Illustrations © Thomas Nelson & Sons Ltd; Photographs © as listed on p.2, sourced texts on p.44. Published by Thomas Nelson & Sons Ltd 1999.

20 March

The first concentration camp opens at Dachau, near Munich. Its initial purpose is to house arrested communists and other left-wing opponents of the Nazi regime. In the future it will be used to detain and ultimately murder Jews.

28 March

The Nazi press agitates for a boycott of Jewish shops, doctors and lawyers. Historians have identified various radical groups (such as sections of the SA) and certain individuals (such as Goebbels, the jurist Roland Freisler and the virulently anti-Semitic Julius Streicher, a leading Nazi based in Nuremberg) who were at the centre of this and subsequent initiatives. Their interpretation has been that Hitler was now facing other imperatives and that radicals within the movement had to agitate for the anti-Semitic measures which Hitler had promised in his earlier speeches. Some elements in the party speak privately of Hitler having come to terms with the establishment, having lost the violent edge of his pre-Chancellery days. However, on 29 March Hitler informs his cabinet of the boycott and tells them that he himself had called for it. He terms the boycott 'spontaneous popular violence'. Goebbel's diary entries for the end of March reveal his excitement and show him consulting with Hitler on the timing and duration of the boycott.

1 April

A nationwide boycott of Jewish shops is abandoned after one day. The general public reaction is one of indifference. It becomes apparent that the boycott is incompatible with the stated priority of economic recovery. It soon becomes clear to Hitler and his colleagues that further boycotts can only damage the fragile German economy. However, over the next few months many top firms part company with Jewish members at boardroom level.

Meanwhile a number of eminent Jewish musicians leave the country. The new president of the Prussian Theatre Commission calls them 'Jewish artistic bankrupters'. The Dresden Opera House dismisses its musical director on the grounds that he has too many Jewish contacts. It is the Jewish contribution to culture which is first to be seriously restricted by the new regime.

7 April

Law for the Restoration of the Professional Civil Service excludes Jews and other political opponents. The detailed legislation is drawn up by Wilhelm Frick. Meanwhile widespread outbreaks of violence against Jewish judges, lawyers and jurists leads Hitler to agree to a decree restricting Jews from practising law. This time the initiative stems from the state secretary at the Ministry of Justice. Hitler appears to be reacting to initiatives which in turn stemmed from localised attacks against the Jews. At the same time Hitler personally defers action against Jewish physicians, partly because he recognises that action in this area will impact upon German patients.

25 April

Law Against the Over-Crowding of German Schools restricts the number of Jewish students allowed to enter German schools. Meanwhile action is taken to exclude Jewish professors and academics from university faculties.

10 May

Goebbels is at the centre of a campaign which leads to over 20,000 books by Jews and left-wing writers being thrown onto bonfires in Berlin. Goebbels addresses a large crowd outside the Kroll Opera House in which he condemns Jewish culture. Similar events are staged in every other large German city.

7 July

Hess informs his colleagues that further boycotts of Jewish department stores will not be permitted. Hitler's commitment to economic recovery and his acute sense of his own image with the German people makes him extremely wary of jeopardising his own popularity. One interpretation sees Hitler as holding back the violent radicals in his movement who are itching for action against the Jews.

14 July

At a cabinet meeting, with Hitler present, it is decided not to withhold contracts from Jewish firms. Hitler's priority is to deliver to the German people the economic recovery which he has promised. On the same day the Law for the Prevention of Genetically Diseased Offspring is adopted. This makes it possible to sterilise anyone suffering from hereditary diseases. The eugenic rationale behind such measures is of relevance to the Jews.

By the end of July over 26,000 Germans, including a large number of Jews, have been arrested and taken to concentration camps. In August a small number of Jews are killed.

September

Jews are banned from owning farms or practising agriculture.

4 October

Jews are banned from holding the post of newspaper editor. Meanwhile new disciplinary procedures are implemented at Dachau, including the ruling that from now on 'agitators are to be hanged'.

By the end of the month thousands of placards have appeared across the country in towns, villages and various public places saying, 'Jews are not welcome here'. In some areas the names of Jewish soldiers are removed from war memorials.

December

By the end of the year, 36 Jews have been murdered, a further six killed in 'mob outrages' and three others killed attempting escape. More than 35,000 Jews have fled the country.

TASK

Here are two interpretations of the anti-Semitic programme of 1933:

- a Hitler centred programme;
- a programme restrained by Hitler.

Using the material provided here and your own further reading, explain which you feel is most accurate.

Challenging History Resource Pack. Text © John Traynor; Illustrations © Thomas Nelson & Sons Ltd; Photographs © as listed on p.2, sourced texts on p.44. Published by Thomas Nelson & Sons Ltd 1999.

The concentration camp system

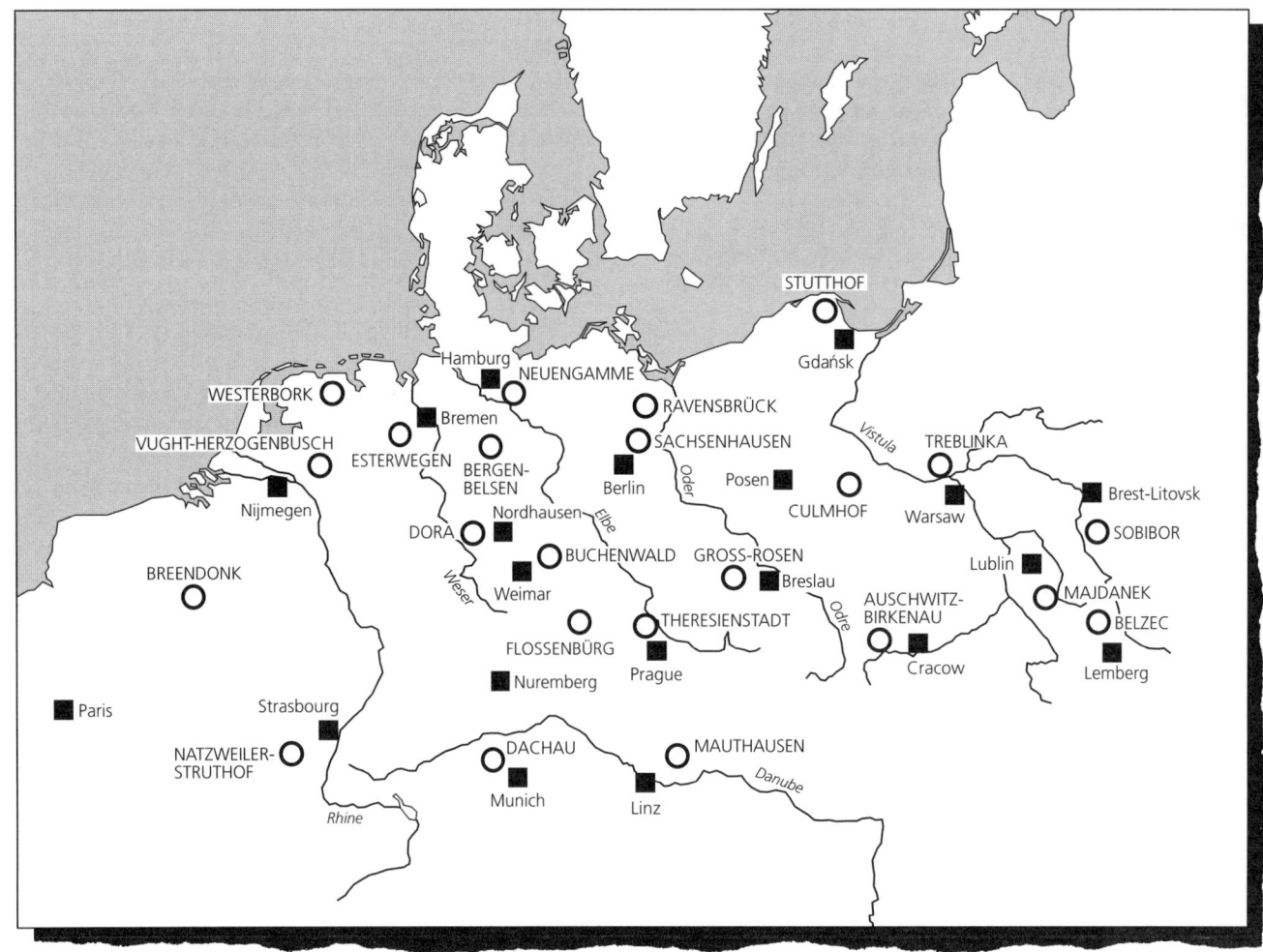

Towards the Holocaust

Historians have been divided as to Hitler's policy towards the Jews. Some historians – the so-called intentionalists – have claimed that Hitler fully intended to take action against the Jews as soon as the opportunity presented itself. They draw a straight and unswerving line through Hitler's virulent anti-Semitism stemming from his time in Vienna, his trauma and desire for revenge after the gas attack in 1918, the setting out of anti-Semitic and foreign policy in *Mein Kampf* in 1924–25, the detailed and systematic anti-Jewish legislation of 1933–39, the murderous policies employed in Poland from 1939 and especially the holocaust unleashed in eastern Europe after the invasion of the Soviet Union in June 1941. The sheer enormity of the crime, combined with Hitler's numerous expressions of vicious intent, have convinced some people that he had always intended to carry out a wholesale campaign against the Jews. This view places Hitler permanently at the centre of a steadily escalating programme, energetically and purposefully implementing a range of policies against the Jews.

It is probably fair to say that a larger number of historians have rejected this approach. The functionalists see the policy as something haphazard. Where some historians have seen a straight road, they have seen a twisted path. They argue that when Hitler came into power on 30 January, he did not have a clear idea or plan as to what to do about the Jews. This view sees Hitler as no less guilty in a moral sense for what happened to the Jews. However, instead of someone setting out a clear line of policy, they see Hitler as an indecisive character, dealing with diverse factions within his own party. They argue that when Hitler became Chancellor he was very conscious of his public image, and acutely aware of his responsibilities concerning the revival of the German economy. They agree that there is no doubt about the extent of Hitler's anti-Semitic feelings, but they claim that even as late as 1939 Hitler had still not arrived at the policy decisions which would set the Holocaust in motion.

The chronology which follows illustrates how the position of the Jews steadily deteriorated from 1935 onwards. Read the outline of events and decide whether this constituted a clear, pre-conceived programme.

Challenging History Resource Pack. Text © John Traynor; Illustrations © Thomas Nelson & Sons Ltd; Photographs © as listed on p.2, sourced texts on p.44. Published by Thomas Nelson & Sons Ltd 1999.

1935

21 May Military Service Act makes 'Aryan descent' a pre-requisite for military service.

Summer Josef Goebbels, the most outspokenly anti-Semitic of Hitler's senior colleagues, pushes for fresh initiatives against the Jews.

September During the Nuremberg rally, Hitler, without consulting colleagues, instructs civil servant Bernhard Losener to immediately draft new laws to prohibit sexual relations between Jews and non-Jews.

15 September Promulgation of the Nuremberg Laws forbidding Jews the status of Reich citizenship. Marriage and sexual relations between Jews and non-Jews are outlawed through the Law for the Protection of German Blood and German Honour.

1936

Summer Anti-Semitic propaganda is repressed for the duration of the Olympic Games in Berlin.

1937

On at least three occasions Hitler personally defers new anti-Semitic measures because of technical or legal objections.

14 March Pope Pius XI criticises Nazi racial policy in his encyclical statement 'with burning concern'.

1938

12 March German troops march into Austria.

9 June Munich's largest synagogue is pulled down.

25 July New restrictions imposed on Jewish doctors.

10 August Nuremberg's synagogue is destroyed.

17 August All Jews in Germany are obliged to add the forenames 'Sara' or 'Israel' to their name.

27 September Jewish lawyers are forbidden to practise.

28 October Deportation of 17,000 Jews of Polish nationality to Poland.

7 November A young Jew, Herschel Grynszpan, shoots and fatally wounds Ernst vom Roth, a German official at the Paris embassy.

9 to 10 November Reichkristalnacht – 'the night of the broken glass'. A pogrom on a national scale results in the murder of 91 Jews, the burning of 191 synagogues and the ransacking of more than 7,000 Jewish shops. Around 30,000 Jews are arrested and imprisoned. The pogrom is not marked by any particular policy decision or decisive meeting. However, in the words of historian Daniel Goldhagen, 'the nationwide pogrom…was an event of enormous significance. The Germans' measures taken until then had not succeeded in completely removing the Jews from their country, so it was time to become more severe, to send an unmistakable message and warning; Leave, or else'.

1939

30 January On the sixth anniversary of his coming to power Hitler delivers a venomous speech to the Reichstag predicting the future annihilation of the Jewish race. (See documents.)

14 to 15 March German troops occupy Czechoslovakia.

1 September Germany invades Poland. Special SS units accompany the regular troops. They display great brutality towards the Polish Jews but killings are generally confined to the leaders of the Jewish community.

6 October Conquest of Poland complete.

12 to 17 October Jews deported from Austria and Czechoslovakia to Poland.

18 November Through his military adjutant, Hitler dismisses concerns amongst sections of the Army leadership about the violence of the anti-Jewish policy as 'childish'.

23 November Polish Jews obliged to wear the yellow Star of David.

December Officials planning Poland's future discuss the destruction of Jewish 'sub humanity' living in the ghettos.

1940

Early in the year it is decided to place the Jews of Lodz in a ghetto in the northern part of the city. In April the ghetto is sealed, trapping 164,000 Jews inside.

3 July Discussion takes place of the Madagascar Plan – to place the Jews on an island off the coast of Africa. Some historians interpret this as a sign that the decision to launch the 'Final Solution' has still not been arrived at.

1941

17 to 30 March In a military conference Hitler tells his generals that the campaign in Russia will be a war of annihilation.

22 June Germany invades the Soviet Union.

23 June The Einsatzgruppen (mobile SS units – 'Action Squads') advance into Russia.

2 July Heydrich instructs the Einsatzgruppen to 'execute Jews in the service of the Party or the State'. In the first instance it appears that women and children were generally excluded from executions.

31 July Goering signs authorisation to Heydrich (see documents). This document is seen by some historians as of vital importance in the launching of the 'Final Solution'.

August Himmler visits the east to witness the killings but reports that he is worried about the 'burden' this places on German soldiers.

mid-August Sudden commencement of execution of Jewish children in Russia.

1 September German Jews obliged to wear the yellow Star of David. In the same month, 33,371 Jews are murdered by the Einsatzgruppen at Babi Yar, on the outskirts of Kiev in the Ukraine.

14 October Order passed to move Jews from Reich territory to the eastern ghettos.

15 October to 11 November Twenty trains leave the Third Reich carrying Jews to Lodz.

29 November High-ranking civil servants and bureaucrats are invited to a conference at Wannsee on 9 December 1941, later postponed to 20 January 1942.

December First use of 'gas vans' for mass execution of Jews at Chelmno in Poland.

By the end of the year it had been decided that the camp at Auschwitz could not cope with the volume of prisoners being sent there and so Auschwitz II – Birkenau – was built. It became the largest Nazi extermination camp. It is estimated that eventually one million Jews were gassed there.

1942

20 January Wannsee Conference in Berlin. Detailed discussion of the bureaucratic and organisational details of the 'Final Solution' led by Heydrich.

July 1942 Mass executions begin at Treblinka in Poland. 800,000 Jews are killed there by August 1943, under the administration of just 50 Germans and 150 Ukrainians.

Winter Polish Catholics form the Zegota, a group aiming to provide safe areas for Jewish children.

TASKS

Essays

1 Why did the position of European Jewry deteriorate so markedly between 1935–42?

2 To what extent was the worsening situation of the Jews due to the personal intervention of Adolf Hitler?

3 'The Reichkristalnacht of November 1938 was the turning point for the Jews' – how far would you agree with this view?

Challenging History Resource Pack. Text © John Traynor; Illustrations © Thomas Nelson & Sons Ltd; Photographs © as listed on p.2, sourced texts on p.44. Published by Thomas Nelson & Sons Ltd 1999.

Contemporary sources

Source A

If I am ever really in power the destruction of the Jews will be my first and most important job. As soon as I have the power, I shall have gallows after gallows erected…Then the Jews will be hanged one after another…until Germany is cleansed of the last Jew.

Adolf Hitler, extract from a letter written in 1922

Source C

Out with them [the Jews] from all the professions and into the ghettos with them! Fence them in somewhere where they can finish as they deserve while the German people look on the way people stare at wild animals.

Hitler's comment to close colleagues at the end of the
Nuremberg rally in September 1935

Source D

One thing I should like to say on this day which may be memorable for others as well as for us Germans. In the course of my life I have very often been a prophet, and have usually been ridiculed for it. During the time of my struggle for power it was in the first instance only the Jewish race that received my prophesies with laughter when I said that I would one day take over the leadership of the State, and with it that of the whole nation, and that I would then among other things settle the Jewish problem. Their laughter was uproarious, but I think that for some time now they have been laughing on the other side of their face. Today I will once more be a prophet; if the international Jewish financiers in and outside Europe should succeed in plunging the nations once more into a world war, then the result will not be the Bolshevizing of the earth, and thus the victory of Jewry, but the annihilation of the Jewish race in Europe!

Extract from Hitler's speech to the Reichstag, 30 January 1939

Source F

Communism is a tremendous danger for the future. We must get away from the standpoint of soldierly comradeship. The Communist is from first to last no comrade. It is a war of extermination. If we do not regard it as such, we may defeat the enemy, but in thirty year's time we will again be confronted by the communist enemy. We are not fighting in a war in order to conserve the enemy.

Summary by General Halder of Hitler's comments to military leaders
at a conference on 30 March 1941

Source B

When we speak of new land in Europe today we must principally bear in mind Russia and the border states subject to her. Destiny itself seems to wish to point the way for us here…for centuries Russia drew nourishment as a State from the Germanic nucleus of its governing classes. But this nucleus has now been almost completely exterminated and destroyed. It has been replaced by the Jew…The colossal empire in the East is ripe for dissolution. And the end of the Jewish domination in Russia will also be the end of Russia as a State. We have been chosen by destiny to be the witnesses of a catastrophe which will afford the strongest confirmation of the soundness of the volkisch theory of race.

Adolf Hitler, *Mein Kampf* (1925)

Source E

With reference to the meeting which took place today in Berlin, I would like to emphasise once again that the overall measures envisaged (i.e. the final goal) must be kept strictly secret. A distinction must be made between.

1   The final goal (which will require a lengthy period) and
2   The stages towards the achievement of this final goal (which can be carried out on a short-term basis)…

It is obvious that the tasks which are desirable cannot be defined in every detail…

1   The first preliminary measure for achieving the final goal is the concentration of the Jews from the countryside in the larger cities…
    As a matter of principle, Jewish communities of under 500 are to be dissolved and transferred to the nearest concentration city…To achieve these goals I expect the absolute commitment of all forces of the Security Police and the Security Service.

Extract from Heydrich's instructions to the Einsatzgruppen regarding
the 'Jewish Question' in the occupied territory of Poland,
21 September 1939

TASKS

1   Use sources **A** to **G** to present a **detailed** case in support of the **intentionalist** view that Hitler planned the Holocaust in a deliberate, systematic fashion from 1933–42. Include detailed reference to key dates, decision-making and turning points in the planning of the Holocaust. Extract quotations from the sources to support your case.

2   What evidence is there to contradict the intentionalist view?

Challenging History Resource Pack. Text © John Traynor; Illustrations © Thomas Nelson & Sons Ltd; Photographs © as listed on p.2, sourced texts on p.44. Published by Thomas Nelson & Sons Ltd 1999.

Source G

To supplement the task that was assigned to you on 24 January 1939, which dealt with the solution of the Jewish problem by emigration and evacuation in the most suitable way, I hereby charge you with making all necessary preparations with regard to organisational, technical and material matters for bringing about a complete solution of the Jewish question within the German sphere of influence in Europe...I request you further to send me, in the near future, an overall plan covering the organisational, technical and material measures necessary for the accomplishment of the final solution of the Jewish question which we desire.

Document signed by Goering on 31 July 1941 and drafted by Heydrich's staff

The views of historians

Source H

The effect of years of research has been that historians have moved away from a picture of Hitler and his closest accomplices stricken with racial mania, making deep-laid plans to translate their fantasies into reality and then implementing these plans with demonic thoroughness, while keeping the fact from public knowledge throughout. Today we know how complex and contradictory were the processes that led to the gradual and growing radicalisation of Nazi racial policies and extermination methods.

Detlev J.K. Peukert, *The Genesis of the Final Solution* (1994)

Source I

By underscoring that Hitler and his ideology had a decisive impact on the course of the regime, I do not mean in any way to imply that Auschwitz was a pre-ordained result of Hitler's accession to power. The anti-Jewish policies of the thirties must be understood in their context, and even Hitler's murderous rage and his scanning of the political horizon for the most extreme options do not suggest the existence of any plans for total extermination in the years prior to the German invasion of the Soviet Union.

Saul Friedlander, *Nazi Gemany and the Jews 1933–1939* (1997)

Source J

The images of the gas chambers would forever shape and define Nazism. But one should not read History backwards...The journey to the gas chambers was not a simple one. Stages along the route included the anti-Semitism engendered in the wake of the World War One defeat; the desire to exclude Jews from German life and the Nazis' belief that Jews were both a dangerous and inferior race: the invasion of Poland, which brought 3 million Polish Jews under Nazi control; and finally the decision to kill Communists and Jews in the wake of Operation Barbarossa. No blueprint for the holocaust existed before 1941: the Nazi regime was too chaotic for that. Above all, it was the invasion of Russia that caused a radical change in the Nazis approach to the Jews.

Laurence Rees, *The Nazis: A Warning from History* (1997)

Source K

In mid-March of 1942, some 75 to 80 per cent of all victims of the Holocaust were still alive, while some 20 to 25 per cent had already perished. A mere eleven months later, in mid-February 1943 the situation was exactly the reverse. Some 75 to 80 per cent of all Holocaust victims were already dead, and a mere 20 to 25 per cent still clung to a precarious existence. At the core of the Holocaust was an intense eleven-month wave of mass murder. The centre of gravity of this mass murder was Poland, where in March 1942, despite two and a half years of terrible hardship, deprivation, and persecution, every major Jewish community was still intact; eleven months later, only remnants of Polish Jewry survived in a few rump ghettos and labour camps.

Christopher R. Browning, 'One Day in Jozefow, Initiation to Mass Murder' from *Nazism and German Society 1933–1945*, edited by David F. Crew (1994)

TASKS

1 Read sources **H** to **K**. Write a brief summary of the viewpoint of each of the four historians whose views are presented here.

2 How would you categorise the position of each of the historians? Do they represent the intentionalist or structuralist position?

3 **Essay** Read **all** of the material presented here on the development of anti-Semitism. Then explain how far you would agree with the following statements: 'As late as 1940, Hitler remained undecided on the "Jewish Question". It was the invasion of the Soviet Union which transformed the situation.'

Preview

The name of Neville Chamberlain has become synonymous with the controversial policy of appeasement. For the last fifty years, both the man and the strategy he devised to deal with the threat provided by Hitler's foreign policy have been subjected to a vast outpouring of extreme and sometimes simplistic criticism. However, as historian Keith Robbins states: 'Recent writing has had little patience with the simple stereotypes which once dominated the field.'

This unit aims to develop your knowledge of the personality of Neville Chamberlain, the three visits paid by Chamberlain to Hitler and the general crises of 1938–39. It will also enable you to consider the problems and constraints, both domestic and foreign, which were faced by policy makers, and particularly the Prime Minister, at that time.

Neville Chamberlain returns to England after the Munich Conference and waves the now famous 'piece of paper' to a relieved crowd at Heston airport. This photograph came, more than any other, to symbolise the policy of appeasement.

TASKS

Instructions

The objective throughout this exercise is to decide, working in small groups, what you would have done had you been assigned the task of responding to Hitler's aggressive foreign policy at key points in 1938–39.

- Read through Section A which gives the background briefing notes concerning Case 1 – Anschluss with Austria, March 1938 (the union between Germany and Austria).

- Then study and discuss Section B – the foreign policy options (**a** to **h**) concerning the Anschluss.

- Consider your initial preferences at this stage.

- Once you have made your initial judgement look for the first time at Section C which outlines the constraints faced by the makers of foreign policy at that time.

- Discuss how the constraints have changed your opinions.

- Next, consider the primary sources and the further problems they suggest.

- You now need to present a paper to the other groups in which you set out a clear and logical policy decision. Your group will need to:
  (a) outline the options you considered initially;
  (b) explain the impact of the constraints and the primary sources upon your choices;

(c) select
  (i) a single option
  (ii) a combination of options
  (iii) a sequence of options, e.g. a warning and, if this is not heeded, then mobilisation followed by war.

You will need to be able to explain and justify your decisions and answer questions.

Now repeat this exercise with regard to Case 2 – the Sudetenland – and then, finally, Case 3 – from Czechoslovakia to Poland.

Conclusion

1 What was your group's original attitude towards Chamberlain and appeasement?

2 Compare the line of policy you took to the policy followed at the time. What differences are there? Have you acted with hindsight?

3 To what extent have your views of Chamberlain changed?

4 Consider the views of historians and their verdicts on the policy of appeasement.

5 **Essay** Why was Hitler's Foreign Policy programme between 1938 and 1939 not more effectively

Challenging History Resource Pack. Text © John Traynor; Illustrations © Thomas Nelson & Sons Ltd; Photographs © as listed on p.2, sourced texts on p.44. Published by Thomas Nelson & Sons Ltd 1999.

Section A: background briefing notes – steps to war

Case 1: Anschluss with Austria, March 1938

- Hitler had stated in *Mein Kampf* that 'German-Austria must be restored to the German Motherland', 'because people of the same blood should be in the same Reich'.
- German troops entered Austria on 11 March 1938.
- On 13 March, Austria was declared part of the Reich.
- This followed concerted pressure on the Austrian Chancellor throughout February and March.
- The Austrian armed forces offered no resistance.
- The people of Austria appeared to give Hitler a rapturous reception.
- Italy, which had mobilised troops in Austria's defence in 1934, took no action on this occasion.
- This action was in clear breach of the Treaty of Versailles, although rearmament and the reoccupation of the Rhineland had provided earlier breaches.
- The move had been greeted enthusiastically in Germany.
- There appeared to be little public disapproval in Britain.

Case 2: the Sudetenland, September 1938

- Even before the Czech crisis began, senior British politicians had little loyalty to the Czech state. This country was regarded as a highly artificial creation, and Churchill said that the whole Czech settlement was 'an affront to self-determination'.
- Flushed with the success of the Anschluss and encouraged by the lack of any response from the powers, Hitler now turned his attention to the substantial German minority of three and half million in the Sudetenland.
- The Anschluss had clearly made the position of Czechoslovakia more vulnerable.
- Although Britain had no agreement with the Czechs, the French did. However, a difference of opinion between the French premier, Daladier, and his Foreign Minister, Bonnet, meant that it was never really clear whether France would resort to military action on Czechoslovakia's behalf.
- Czechoslovakia carried out major military preparations in order to defend her borders.
- German pressure on the Czech government mounted through the summer of 1938, intensified by stories of atrocities committed by the Czechs against the Sudeten Germans.
- Through the Minister Lord Runciman, Britain attempted to resolve the problem through diplomatic negotiation with the Czechs. However, with the Sudeten Germans demanding autonomy, Hitler renounced these negotiations.
- On 15 September 1938, Chamberlain set off for his first meeting with Hitler at Berchtesgaden. Chamberlain agreed to discuss self-determination with the Cabinet upon his return to London, with the proviso that Hitler would not pre-empt this with an invasion.
- Chamberlain returned to Germany to meet Hitler at Bad Godesberg. Although Chamberlain had proposals which seemed to meet Hitler's main demands, the Prime Minister was stunned to find Hitler in truculent mood, threatening immediate German military occupation of the Sudetenland. In addition, Hitler now emphasised the rights of the other minority groups in the Sudetenland. The only concession Chamberlain was able to obtain from Hitler was a slight delay in the military timetable. Though Chamberlain was appalled by Hitler's behaviour, he now seemed convinced that successful resolution of this issue could mark a turning point in Anglo-German relations.
- Chamberlain now sought Cabinet approval for accession to Hitler's demands. It was now that deep divisions in the Cabinet began to emerge.
- France and Czechoslovakia wanted to reject Hitler's terms in the wake of the Bad Godesberg meeting.
- Chamberlain sent Sir Horace Wilson to see Hitler to discuss the formation of an international body.
- While Wilson was away, Chamberlain broadcast to the nation on the night of 27 September 1938 his willingness 'to pay even a third visit to Germany' because of the 'horrible, fantastic, incredible' fact that Britain was preparing for war 'because of a quarrel in a far-away country between people of whom he knew nothing'.
- Via Wilson, Chamberlain proposed an Anglo-German conference. Hitler responded with an invitation to Munich.
- At the conference the Sudetenland was ceded to Germany. In return, Chamberlain received guarantees on the integrity of rump Czechoslovakia and obtained Hitler's signature on the 'piece of paper', which promised that future disputes would be resolved by discussion and negotiation.

Challenging History Resource Pack. Text © John Traynor; Illustrations © Thomas Nelson & Sons Ltd; Photographs © as listed on p.2, sourced texts on p.44. Published by Thomas Nelson & Sons Ltd 1999.

Case 3: from Czechoslovakia to Poland, March 1939

- In the wake of the Munich conference, Chamberlain was swept along by a short-lived but rapturous reception. He seemed to have averted the threat of war.

- Intelligence reports soon began to suggest that Hitler was dissatisfied with Munich.

- The violent anti-Semitic pogrom in Germany in November 1938 heightened the feeling that Hitler was not a man to reason with and that Chamberlain's obsessive sense of mission had blinded him to the real nature of the dictator.

- On 15 March 1939, German troops entered Prague and established a 'Protectorate of Bohemia and Moravia', while Slovakia was declared 'independent but under German protection'. Hitler had clearly gone beyond his stated aims of including all Germans in one German nation. It was now apparent that Hitler's promises meant nothing.

- A drastic change in opinion towards appeasement now took place. As William Rock says: 'Nearly everywhere the reduction of Munich to utter mockery was seen as totally discrediting appeasement and finally compelling its abandonment.' This hostile view spread through the public, in all sections of the British press, parliament and the foreign office. Chamberlain's statement in the Commons that Britain should not 'be deflected from our course' provoked widespread anger.

- In March 1939, Britain and France promised aid to Poland in the event of a threat to Polish independence. In April, this guarantee was extended to Romania and Greece.

- Britain now entered – to the deep suspicion of Poland – into protracted negotiations with Russia. These were dramatically curtailed with the announcement of the Nazi-Soviet Non-Aggression pact on 22 August 1939.

- Britain now reaffirmed her guarantee to Poland, but at the same time tried to bring about negotiations between Germany and Poland. Hitler showed no interest in this.

- On 1 September 1939, Germany invaded Poland.

- For two days Britain wavered over the guarantee but, after bitter scenes in the Commons and an outraged response by several ministers, Britain finally declared war on Germany on 3 September 1939.

  Chamberlain now said that he would be ready to negotiate with Germany if the invasion was halted and German troops withdrawn. As William Rock says, this shows 'his nearly indestructible attachment to the idea of a negotiated settlement with Germany which might yet bring European stability'.

The invasion of Poland: German troops opening up a border crossing, 1 September 1939.

Challenging History Resource Pack. Text © John Traynor; Illustrations © Thomas Nelson & Sons Ltd; Photographs © as listed on p.2, sourced texts on p.44. Published by Thomas Nelson & Sons Ltd 1999.

Contemporary sources

Source A

We have but a facade of imperial defence. The whole structure is unsound.

Maurice Hankey, the Cabinet Secretary (1934), quoted in R. Overy, *The Road to War* (1989)

Source B

[British post-war governments] had to choose between, on the one hand, a policy of disarmament, social reforms and…financial rehabilitation, and on the other hand, a heavy expenditure on armaments. Under a powerful impulse for development every government of every party elected for the former.

Stanley Baldwin, the Prime Minister (1936), quoted in R. Overy, *The Road to War* (1989)

Source C

So far as commitments on the continent are concerned, the services can only take note of them.

Extract from a report by Chiefs of Staff (1926), quoted in R. Overy, *The Road to War* (1989)

Source D

Armed conflict between nations is a nightmare to me but if I were convinced that any nation had made up its mind to dominate the world by fear of its force, I should feel that it must be resisted.

Neville Chamberlain, Prime Minister, for a Radio broadcast of 1938, quoted in R. Overy, *The Road to War* (1989)

Source E

[Czechoslovakia was not an issue] on which we would be on very strong ground for plunging Europe into war.

Alexander Cadogan, Head of the Foreign Office, quoted in R. Overy, *The Road to War* (1989)

Source F

[There would be no point in fighting Germany] unless we had a reasonable prospect of being able to beat her to her knees in a reasonable time and of that I see no sign.

Chamberlain, quoted in R. Overy, *The Road to War* (1989)

The views of historians

Source G

Chamberlain was not an ignorant meddler in matters in which he had no experience. When he became Prime Minister he seemed at the time to be the only man for the job. Churchill praised him fulsomely when seconding his nomination for the Conservative Party leadership. Neville was 'efficient and energetic'.

Keith Robbins, *Appeasement* (1988)

Source H

In 1939 Chamberlain introduced in the annual budget an extensive four year plan for rearmament, which provided the framework for the military structure with which Britain entered the war in 1939…Far from failing to rearm, the government was accused of rearming 'on a gigantic scale', and with 'feverish haste'. It is forgotten that Chamberlain, man of peace that he was, did not exclude the possibility of war…Chamberlain as Chancellor of the Exchequer had played the leading part in the development of Britain's rearmament programme from 1936 onwards.

R. Overy, *The Road to War* (1989)

Source I

Nor was Neville Chamberlain in any way attracted to Nazism or beguiled by Hitler himself, though he rashly gave reason to believe that he was when he referred publicly to Hitler having pledged his word. He had been at the centre of the British rearmament effort since its inception in 1934 and had urged and pressed it forward…There is abundant evidence to show he doubted and distrusted Hitler's sincerity at every turn. He was relentless…impelled always to act and to decide and never afraid of taking an unwelcome or unpopular decision. For those who were not as he was, who opposed him, he had little but contempt,… Chamberlain dominated his Cabinet.

Donald Cameron Watt, *How War Came* (1989)

Section B: foreign policy options – the problems and constraints of diplomacy

Case 1: Austria, March 1938

(N.B. in the immediate aftermath of the Anschluss.)

a   Immediate full-scale military action by Britain, perhaps with French backing.

b   Some form of mobilisation, either full or partial.

c   Try to initiate action through the League. Sanctions or moral condemnation.

d   Issue a firm warning. Set a precise time limit to further action.

e   Diplomatic condemnation/criticism. Withdrawal of diplomats from Berlin.

f   Diplomatic initiative. Some form of conference. Participants to be determined.

g   Do nothing. Wait and see. Meanwhile, step up rearmament/civil defence.

h   Other option. Please specify.

Case 2: the Sudetenland, September 1938

(N.B. Hitler is agitating for the addition of the Sudetenland to the Reich, but has not yet taken any action.)

a   The Czechs have already mobilised. Give them full support.

b   Provide limited aid to the Czechs in their defence of the Sudetenland, e.g. arms.

c   Warn Hitler that if he takes action against the Czechs, Britain will step in, and perhaps France.

d   Diplomatic resistance/criticism/condemnation.

e   Urge the Czechs to cede the Sudetenland.

f   Conference: (i) Britain, Germany, France, Italy; (ii) as with (i) plus Czechs and/or Russians.

g   Do nothing. Wait and see. Meanwhile, step up rearmament/civil defence.

h   Other option. Please specify.

Case 3: Czechoslovakia, March 1939

(N.B. in the immediate aftermath of Hitler's annexation of rump Czechoslovakia.)

a   Czechoslovakia has been over-run. Provide immediate, full-scale military assistance.

b   Provide some form of limited assistance to the Czechs.

c   Some form of mobilisation.

d   Poland now under threat: make formal guarantees to Poland.

e   Poland now under threat: try to make an alliance with Russia.

f   Invite Hitler to a further conference. Participants to be decided.

g   Set Hitler a clear limit to further action, e.g. through **d**.

h   Do nothing. Wait and see. Meanwhile, step up rearmament/civil defence.

i   Other option. Please specify.

Challenging History Resource Pack. Text © John Traynor; Illustrations © Thomas Nelson & Sons Ltd; Photographs © as listed on p.2, sourced texts on p.44. Published by Thomas Nelson & Sons Ltd 1999.

Hitler's foreign policy, 1935–39

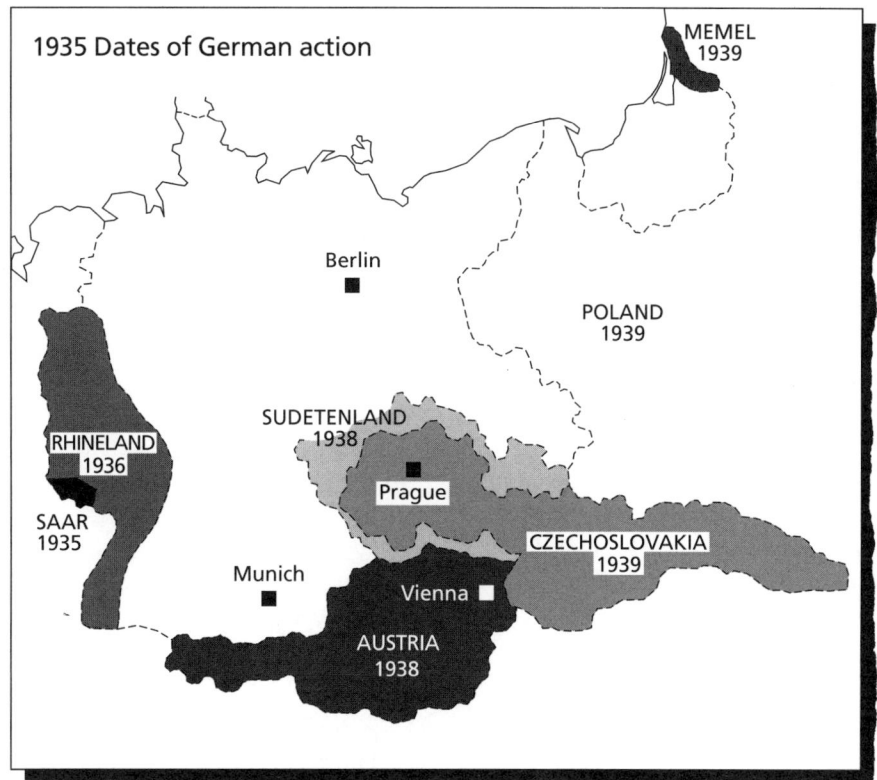

1935 Dates of German action

MEMEL 1939

Berlin

POLAND 1939

SUDETENLAND 1938

RHINELAND 1936

Prague

SAAR 1935

CZECHOSLOVAKIA 1939

Munich

Vienna

AUSTRIA 1938

Section C: constraints

N.B. Read these carefully before making any policy decision. Some constraints are general and will apply at all times. Others are specific to a particular crisis.

- Intelligence reports from the military chiefs of staff suggest that a war with Germany would probably be lengthy, costly (both in terms of casualties and economically) and with no guarantee of the outcome.

- Domestic issues are very pressing. There is a need for major spending on social reforms, e.g. a major housing programme.

- There is a general election forthcoming – the fear is that Labour might triumph if social reforms are delayed.

- There is very little evidence of public support for a war. The mood changes somewhat in the aftermath of Munich and Hitler's invasion of Czechoslovakia.

- Public opinion seems to be that the Anschluss/ Sudetenland are German issues and that Versailles may well have been too harsh in these areas. Indeed Austria is seen as 'in Hitler's own backyard'.

- Hitler states publicly after each of Cases 1, 2 and 3 that he has no further territorial aims. Many people believe this to be the case, although after Case 3 there is also a strong feeling that he can no longer be trusted.

- There is an intense feeling of 'never again' after the horrors of 1914.

- Italy, which had in 1934 been Austria's guarantor, had since:
  (i) invaded Abyssinia; (ii) been criticised by the League; (iii) moved towards Hitler; (iv) turned a blind eye towards the Anschluss.

- Cases 2 and 3 raise the issue of the role of the Soviet Union. But British stance since the Bolshevik revolution has been generally hostile. There is a feeling that Stalin cannot be trusted. If Russian help is to be enlisted regarding either the Czech or Polish frontiers, then the Poles would need to give consent to Russian troop movements. However, the Poles regard the Russians with suspicion and they are wary of the West.

- France has made guarantees towards the Czechs, but then they are worried that they may be left on their own to defend the Czechs.

- There is grave concern in Britain that a war with Hitler might lead to heavy civilian casualties because civil defences are very limited. Time and money will be needed to improve this area.

- The credibility of the League has been gravely damaged by the events.

Sources

Browning, Christopher 'One day in Jozefow, initiation to mass murder' in David F Crew (ed), *Nazism and German Society 1933–1945* (1994) Routledge

Bullock, Alan *Hitler and Stalin: parallel lives* (1991) HarperCollins Publishers Ltd

Cameron Watt, Donald *How War Came* (1989) Heinemann

Caplan, Jane 'The Rise of National Socialism' from Gordon Martel (ed), *Modern Germany Reconsidered 1870–1945* (1992) Routledge

Carr, William *Hitler: a study in personality and politics* (1978) Edward Arnold

de Jonge, Alex *Stalin and the Shaping of the Soviet Union* (1986) Fontana, HarperCollins Publishers Ltd

Fest, Joachim *Hitler* (1974) Weidenfeld & Nicolson

Friedlander, Saul *Nazi Germany and the Jews 1933–1939* (1997), Weidenfeld & Nicolson

Getty, J. Arch *Origins of the Great Purges* (1985) Cambridge University Press

Hamann, Brigitte *Hitler's Wein* (1996) R. Piper (translated as *Hitler's Vienna* (1999) Oxford University Press)

Kershaw, Ian *Hitler: Profiles in Power* (1991) Longman. Reprinted by permission of Addison Wesley Longman Ltd

Lewis, Jonathan & Whitehead, Phillip *Stalin: a time for judgement* (1989) Methuen

McNeal, Robert H. *Stalin, Man and Ruler* (1988) Macmillan

Overy, R. *The Road to War* (1989) Macmillan

Peukert, Detlev J. K. *The Genesis of the Final Solution* (1994) Routledge

Radzinsky, Edvard *Stalin* (1996) Sceptre

Rees, Laurence *The Nazis: a warning from history* (1997) BBC Books. Reproduced with permission of BBC Worldwide Limited. © Laurence Rees

Robbins, Keith *Appeasement* (1988) Blackwell Publishers

Rock, William *British Appeasement in the 1930s* (1978) Edward Arnold

Zubok, Vladislav & Pleshakov, Constantine *Inside the Kremlin's Cold War: from Stalin to Kruschev* (1996) Harvard University Press. Copyright © 1996 by the Fellows and Trustees of Harvard College. Reprinted by permission of Harvard University Press